F4U CORSAIR AT WAR

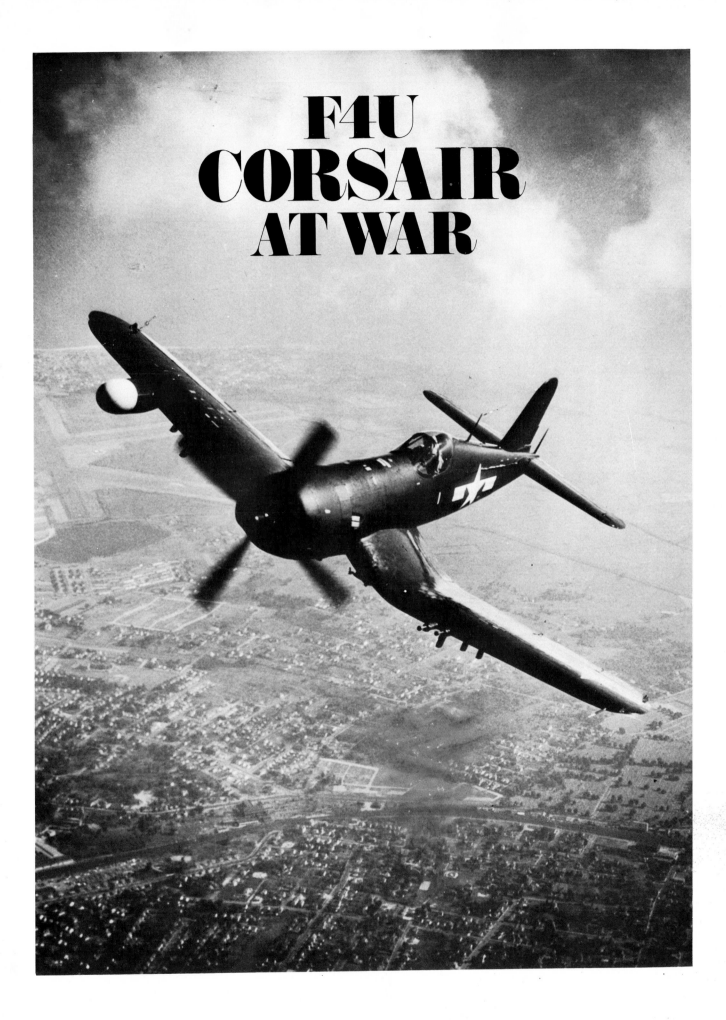

F4U CORSAIR AT WAR

Richard Abrams

LONDON
IAN ALLAN LTD

First published 1977

ISBN 0 7110 0766 7

Design by Anthony Wirkus LSIAD

© Richard Abrams 1977

Published by Ian Allan Ltd, Shepperton, Surrey,
and printed in the United Kingdom by
Ian Allan Printing Ltd

Contents

Foreword
Colonel Gregory 'Pappy' Boyington, USMC (Ret.)

Corsair at War has to be considered a first in aviation history for two reasons. Until now, there has not been a substantive book of any type published that describes the long, distinguished history of the Corsair. Look around — you can find many books on fighters such as the North American P-51 Mustang, the Supermarine Spitfire, the Focke-Wulf Fw190, the Messerschmitt Bf109 and many others, but nothing about the US Marine Corps' most famous prop-driven fighter, the Chance Vought F4U Corsair. Additionally, any story of a great airplane is best told by the people who actually flew it in combat, not by someone who has tried to interpret what it was like to do so. I am honoured to be able to contribute in a small way to help tell the story of the Corsair, along with other pilots who fought in combat in this great fighter.

This book relates the operational history of the Corsair from its conception in 1938, through World War II, the Korean conflict, and beyond into the war in Indo China. I must say, however, that the Corsair's greatest day was when the US Navy decided that the airplane was not suitable for use as a carrier fighter, but would instead be relegated to land-based US Marine Corps fighter pilots in the South Pacific. From that day until the end of World War II, and again during the Korean Conflict, it was proven first by the US Marine Corps, and finally by the US Navy, that the Corsair was indeed a great airplane. The French also knew this and the Corsair served them well into the sixties, which is an honourable record for an airplane that was designed before World War II. The fact that the airplane still endures can be seen every week when a small number of well-maintained Corsairs are used in a National Broadcasting Company (NBC) television series that dramatises the exploits of my World War II US Marine Corps fighter squadron, the 'Black Sheep', VMF-214.

Lest we forget this book, it is a story of the Corsair that is essentially told by the men who flew the airplane, with just enough technical information included to bring the airplane's progressive development into perspective. I am proud to be a part of the Corsair's history and appreciate this opportunity to be able to join with others and relate first-hand experiences of what it was like to fly a Corsair at war.

March 1977
Fresno, California

Above: Major Gregory 'Pappy' Boyington, USMC. */US National Archives*

Left: Corsairs of VMF-214 'Black Sheep' over Bougainville, in the Solomon Islands, February 1944./*US National Archives*

Col. Gregory "Pappy" Boyington

Introduction

The Vought Corsair is forever engraved in aviation history as the last, and probably the finest propeller-driven combat fighter airplane. Each of the Services of the United States and Great Britain made a fighter great in World War II, and history will never forget the US Air Force's North American P-51 Mustang, the US Navy's Grumman F6F Hellcat, the Royal Air Force's Supermarine Spitfire, and most certainly, the US Marine Corps' Vought F4U Corsair.

Under the all too familiar hectic pressures of the war, the US Navy grew impatient with the Corsair because of its poor carrier landing characteristics, and instead, concentrated on the development of the Grumman F6F Hellcat as its standard carrier fighter. The Marine Corps, whose equipment consisted wholly of what it was assigned by the Navy, had the Corsair handed over to it, for better or for worse. Marine pilots got 'the word' that Navy pilots had found the Corsair too difficult to handle aboard carriers, and as a consequence, had retreated from it in awe. This half-truth generated an affection for the Corsair among the Marine pilots from the start, and it grew like a disease. During the Korean conflict, the Marine Corps and Navy operated Corsairs from carriers, while the Grumman F6F, and even the highly touted Grumman F8F Bearcat, remained on state-side duty in reserve units.

The Corsair was still rolling off the assembly lines more than ten years after the first production airplane was delivered, and fourteen years after the start of its design. While this is not a record per se (other aircraft have had longer production runs), it is an unbelievable record for a combat aircraft in the most competitive of design fields, that of the fighter.

Two things are required to create the rare environment in which a seemingly ageless aircraft can exist. First, it must be a very good airplane. Second, the peculiar tactical situation into which it was born must persist. The Corsair met both of these criteria. It was one of the fastest propeller-driven aircraft in the world, and its unmatched versatility included the ability to perform in the close air support role that was so vital to the successful conduct of World War II, and later, the Korean conflict.

This volume is not intended to give a detailed technical analysis of the Corsair, nor is it meant to be a complete operational history of everything that the Corsair achieved in its long service life as a fighter and fighter-bomber in the US Marine Corps, US Navy, Britain's Royal Navy, Royal New Zealand Air Force, and France's Aéronavale. (The Corsair's subsequent role in the service of Argentina, and later in San Salvador and Honduras — where the Corsair is reported to be still flying — will not be covered in this volume.) It has been my goal to describe some of the highlights of the Corsair's career in the various services in which it saw active duty, as well as to relate the little known story of the Corsair night fighter operations during World War II. Much of this is related through the words of the men who flew in these actions. A number of the narratives contained in the Night Fighting Corsair Chapter were taken from official US Marine Corps and Navy aircraft action reports. Elsewhere throughout this volume, I have included verbatim excerpts from official US Navy *Air Operations Memorandum*, which were prepared during World War II by the Commander Air Force, Pacific Fleet. Other narratives have been furnished by a number of former Corsair pilots.

I am extremely indebted to Colonel Gregory 'Pappy' Boyington, USMC (Ret.), first, for his permission to quote from his famous book *Baa Baa Black Sheep*, second, for relating to me his impressions of the Corsair, and finally, for generously volunteering to write the foreword to this volume. My thanks also go to Mrs. Josephine Boyington for her charm, hospitality and wonderful split pea soup. I would also like to express my deep gratitude to Captain John T. 'Tommy' Blackburn, USN (Ret.), who gave me his unpublished manuscript of the history of VF-17 so that I could include a large part of it in this volume. Other narratives have been furnished by a number of former Corsair pilots who have taken the time to dig into their records, and jog their memories in order to relate their important roles in the Corsair's story. In particular I would like to extend my thanks to John Hill, Everette Vaughan, Edward Sovik, Nathan Bedell, Richard Harmer and Lyman Bullard.

Ralph Donnelly of the US Marine Corps Historical Division, Kathleen Lloyd of the Naval Operational Archives Branch, Lee Pearson, Naval Air Systems Command Historian, Clarke Van Vleet of the Naval Aviation History Unit, and Harold Andrews, Technical Consultant to *Naval Aviation News* all did a wonderful job of assisting me in locating the official documentation and much of the research material used in the preparation of this volume. I would also like to thank Lieutenant Commander Barry J. Patterson, Editor of *Approach*, the Naval Aviation Safety Review, for letting me use a large portion of Commander Guy P. Bordelon's article, "A Corsair Pilot Reminisces", from that publication.

Many of the photographs reproduced in this volume were generously provided by Rowland Gill of the US Marine Corps Historical Division, Art Schoeni of Vought Aircraft, Harold Andrews and Jim Sullivan of the American Aviation Historical Society, d'E. C. Darby and John Regan of the Aviation Historical Society of New Zealand, Bernard Millot, John Thistlethwaite, John Hill, Tom Blackburn, Frank Kelly and Lyman Bullard. Gene Boswell very graciously provided me with prints of many of the photographs that were contributed. My thanks to all.

I would also like to express my deepest gratitude to Art Schoeni of Vought Aircraft for his encouragement and assistance, and also for his recommendation to the publisher that I undertake the authorship of *Corsair at War*. Much appreciation also goes to Marianne Hyson and Amy Rodrigues for their indefatigable secretarial assistance. Finally, I would like to thank my wife Pat for her support, encouragement and co-operation which enabled me to complete this volume.

Richard Abrams
Lancaster, California

Below: FAA Corsair Is and IIs (F4U-1s with both 'Birdcage' and raised canopies) in echelon formation./*IWM*

The Birth of the Corsair

The Vought F4U Corsair evolved as a result of a design contest for a new high-speed, single-seat shipboard fighter that was initiated by the US Navy in February 1938. The Chance Vought Aircraft Engineering department, led by Rex B. Beisel, prepared several designs to meet these requirements, and submitted two proposals, designated V-166A and V-166B, to the Navy in April 1938.

The V-166A was to be powered by the Pratt & Whitney R-1830 Twin Wasp, one of the most powerful production radial engines available to the US aircraft industry at that time. The V-166B was a more advanced design that was to be powered by the new air-cooled Pratt & Whitney XR-2800-2 Double Wasp radial engine with a two-stage, two-speed supercharger. Because it was the most powerful engine that would be available

in the foreseeable future, the 2,000hp Double Wasp was an obvious choice, except for the fact that it was an experimental engine, and Pratt & Whitney was under considerable pressure from the US Army Air Corps to concentrate all of their efforts on the development and production of liquid-cooled engines. As a result of strong inter-service rivalry, it was inevitable that since the Air Corps favoured the liquid-cooled inline engine, the Navy would favour the air-cooled radial. That decision was to be fundamental to the success of the Corsair.

The Navy design contest resulted in four widely divergent design proposals. Of these, the V-166B was the most conventional, and at the same time, the most impressive. It was a small fighter, designed around the world's most

Below: The XF4U-1 Corsair mock-up, photographed at the Vought-Sikorsky plant, 11 February 1939.
/Vought Aircraft

powerful air-cooled radial engine, and would require the use of the largest propeller ever used on a fighter. Design approval and a contract for the Corsair prototype aircraft, which was designated XF4U-1, was received by Vought from the Navy on 11 June 1938.

Aerodynamic design of the Corsair began with the selection of the airplane's characteristic inverted gull-wing. This arrangement actually evolved as the optimum solution to a series of design problems. A giant Hamilton Standard 13ft 4in diameter, three-bladed Hydromatic propeller was required to absorb the power of the XR-2800-2 engine. In order to provide blade clearance in the level takeoff attitude, the inverted gull-wing made possible the use of a shorter, sturdier, and lighter weight landing gear than would have been possible with a straight-wing airplane.

Another important reason for using the inverted gull-wing design was aerodynamic. Experiments conducted in the late thirties had shown that the most effective relative position between the airfoil surface and body was a normal or right-angle attachment because this position resulted in minimum interference drag. Application of this simple principle, however, presented practical problems. A straight-wing design dictated that the wing be attached midway between the top and bottom of the fuselage. The inverted gull-wing design permitted a low right-angle attachment between the wing and fuselage, thus maintaining the desired low wing configuration and at the same time, producing the least possible drag.

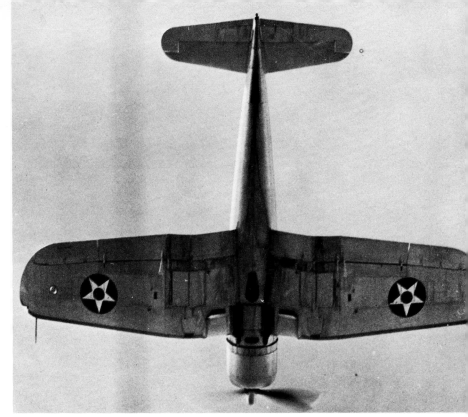

Top: A bottom view of the XF4U-1 showing the 'teardrop' — shaped belly bomb aiming window that was located beneath the cockpit, just aft of the intercooler flap./*USAF*

Above: Clearly shown here are the XF4U-1 Corsair's cowl-mounted 30-calibre machine guns, and wing-mounted 50-calibre machine guns. /*USAF*

Left: The XF4U-1 in the landing configuration showing the prototype's complex deflector plate flaps and drooped ailerons. These features were not incorporated in the production Corsair./*US National Archives*

Additional advantages that resulted from the selection of the inverted gull-wing design were improved pilot visibility because of the low wing, or 'valleys', on either side of the fuselage, and a lower overall height when the wings were folded.

The design of the Corsair was completed and a mock-up of the aircraft was inspected by the Bureau of Aeronautics 8-10 February 1939. Shortly thereafter, construction of the prototype was authorised.

The Corsair was to be the first airplane designed to make virtually exclusive use of new spot welding techniques that had been developed jointly by Vought and the Naval Aircraft Factory. The result was an extremely smooth external finish. Particularly close attention was given to cowling design, and despite the unprecedented heat rejection requirements of the engine, the Corsair featured one of the tightest engine

Below: Vought-Sikorsky Aircraft test pilots, (L to R): Lyman A. Bullard, Jr, Boone T. Guyton, and Frank H. 'Jug' Kelley, Jr. */Lyman Bullard*

cowlings ever designed. Cowl flaps were used to regulate cooling airflow, and the new fighter was the first to use engine exhaust energy for propulsive thrust by incorporating a 'jet thrust' exhaust system.

The original Corsair design specified the use of the Pratt & Whitney XR-2800-2 engine, which could develop 1,800hp at 2,600rpm for takeoff, and 1,500hp at 2,400rpm at 17,500 feet. The -2 engine, however, was eventually delivered to the Navy as an experimental test engine, and instead, an improved XR-2800-4 engine was installed in the XF4U-1. This engine had an increased low blower gear ratio (7.8 versus 6.8 to 1) that resulted in an increase in takeoff power to 1,850hp at 2,600rpm, a normal rated power of 1,600hp at 3,500 feet, and 1,460hp at an altitude of 21,500 feet.

Armament consisted of four machine guns. Two 30-calibre guns (synchronised to fire through the propeller) were mounted in the upper section of the engine compartment with 750 rounds of ammunition per gun. One 50-calibre gun was mounted in each outer wing panel adjacent to the centre section with 300 rounds of ammunition per gun.

Anti-aircraft bombs could be carried in ten compartments, which were located at the mid sections of the outer wing panels. Twenty 5.2lb bombs (four in each of five compartments) could be loaded in each wing panel for a total of 208lbs. A 'teardrop'-shaped belly bomb aiming window was located in the bottom of the fuselage.

Fuel was carried in four integral tanks located in the wing centre sections and outer panel leading edges with total capacity of 273 gallons. The main landing gear struts rotated through 87 degrees as they retracted aft to permit the wheels to lie flat in the wing where they were each completely enclosed by three doors.

After several hours of taxi tests and days of ground engine runs, Lyman A. Bullard, Jr., the Chief of Flight Test at Vought-Sikorsky Aircraft, made the first flight in the prototype XF4U-1 Corsair on 29 May 1940, at the Bridgeport Municipal Airport, Stratford, Connecticut: "As to the first flight of the XF4U-1, that lasted 38 minutes. It was uneventful, just as we had planned it to be. The object of any first flight is to ease the airplane up in the air to a reasonably safe altitude — say 10,000 to 12,000 feet — then gingerly feel out the controls in the clean and partial flap setting conditions, avoiding any abrupt control motions and any actual stall manoeuvres. All that is necessary is

13

Right: The XF4U-1 after Boone Guyton landed it in the rain on the wet fairway at the Norwich Golf Course./*Frank Kelley*

Below: Hoisting the XF4U-1 out of the 'rough'. It took several months to return the prototype Corsair to flight status. /*Frank Kelley*

to get the feel of the airplane so a successful landing can be made, and that is what happened.

"The first two months of the flight test programme were devoted almost solely to engine problems. We had poor fuel distribution from the carburettor causing hot and cold cylinder head temperatures here and there. As a matter of fact, the second pilot to fly the airplane was Pratt & Whitney's Chief Test Pilot, A. Lewis MacLain, so as to confirm my findings and help with the problem since he flew the development programme on the experimental versions of the engine." Flight testing of the new fighter had now begun, and many additional hours of difficult testing would be required before the Corsair was to assume the stature of a first-line fighter.

Shortly after the first flight of the prototype Corsair, Boone T. Guyton assumed test pilot responsibilities for the XF4U-1 flight test effort. While performing a series of low altitude cabin pressurisation tests on the fifth flight of the airplane, he almost contributed to the complete demise of the Corsair programme. It was a murky day with rain showers throughout the Connecticut test area, and Guyton was pressing to complete canopy structure tests that were required in preparation for subsequent high-speed dive tests. After completing a series of high-speed cruise tests, he found himself far to the northeast of the airfield at Stratford, and started to head back to the field realising that his fuel state was low, and that rain showers were probably

heavier than earlier in the day. It wasn't long before he realised that a dense line of rain squalls extended between his position and the airfield.

With fuel extremely low, he started to search for an alternate landing field. With none available in the area, he chose the long fairway at the Norwich Golf Course, after making the decision that he wanted to land before the airplane's fuel supply was completely exhausted, rather than make a dead-stick landing.

Guyton decided that a short carrier-type landing was required and flew the approach with full flaps and power on in order to maintain the slowest possible landing approach speed. As he cut the throttle and allowed the Corsair to settle on to the fairway in the three-point attitude, the wet grass, smooth tyres, and relatively high landing speed (approximately 80 knots) combined to create a highly destructive situation. All of his efforts to bring the aircraft to a stop were futile, and as he neared the edge of the fairway, he tried to ground loop the airplane, but the Corsair's brakes were ineffective on the smooth grass. It hit the rough and crashed into a wooded area at the end of the fairway and was catapulted up by the surrounding trees, flipped over on its back, smashed tail first into the stump of a large tree, and finally stopped halfway down a shallow ravine. Fortunately, when it came to rest, there was enough space for Guyton to crawl from under the open cockpit.

Guyton was uninjured except for small cuts and bruises, and at first it appeared that the mass of crumpled wreckage that was once the XF4U-1 Corsair was a total loss. But everyone soon gained an understanding of the Corsair's rugged construction and the punishment it could withstand. The right wing had been sheared off, the tail assembly badly smashed, and the propeller destroyed. But the main fuselage and engine installation, including the landing gear, were intact. After the airplane was hoisted out of the 'rough', the crew at the Vought experimental hangar started an around-the-clock effort to return the prototype Corsair to flight status. It took several months to complete this task.

The XF4U-1 attained a speed of 405mph during a flight from Stratford to Hartford, Connecticut, on 1 October 1940, becoming the first US fighter to exceed a speed of 400mph in level flight. The Corsair's performance at a time when 400mph was a figure of almost mystical proportion, was final proof that Pratt & Whitney's faith in the air-cooled radial engine was justified. A short time later, Major General Henry H. 'Hap' Arnold, Chief of the Army Air Corps, was told of the Corsair's performance on this flight. This information probably helped influence his decision to give Pratt & Whitney permission to stop development of their liquid-cooled engines, and at the same time, to urge the company to concentrate its efforts on radial engine development.

Further flight testing soon confirmed the outstanding performance capabilities of the XF4U-1. The empty weight of the

Above: The first production F4U-1 Corsair, Bureau of Aeronautics No. 02153, which flew for the first time on 25 June 1942. /*US National Archives*

airplane was only 7,418lbs. It could carry a normal useful load of 2,087lbs (175 gallons of fuel) as a fighter, and 2,295lbs (175 gallons of fuel and 208lbs of anti-aircraft bombs) as a bomber. Maximum useful load as a fighter with maximum fuel (273 gallons) was 2,675lbs. At a normal fighter weight of 9,374lbs, the airplane's sea level rate of climb was 2,600 feet per minute, and its service ceiling was 35,500 feet. Takeoff distance on a calm day was 362 feet, and with a 25-knot headwind, 150 feet. Maximum range of the airplane was 1,040 statute miles at 3,500 feet altitude.

For several reasons, the performance of the prototype XF4U-1 was actually better than predicted. The airplane's exterior surface was finished by smoothing the wing and fuselage surfaces with filler and all openings and skin gaps were sealed. A new Hamilton Standard Hydromatic propeller was installed on the airplane which featured improved efficiency over the type originally selected. In addition, the 'jet thrust' exhaust system and the realisation of very high ram pressure recovery by the wing leading edge carburettor air intakes provided additional performance improvements.

The prototype Corsair was not, however, without shortcomings. The airplane's lateral control system eventually required 96 aileron modifications and 110 test flights before the system was perfected and the airplane's full roll performance capabilities were achieved. The results of wind tunnel spin tests had indicated that

the airplane would have questionable spin recovery characteristics once the spin was fully developed. These predictions were verified during the early phases of the XF4U-1 flight test programme. But, it was felt that this characteristic would not limit the combat performance capabilities of the airplane.

The XF4U-1 was flown to Anacostia Naval Air Station for preliminary Navy flight tests on 24 October 1940. The most objectionable characteristics observed during the early phase of these evaluations was a tendency for the port wing to drop during the landing flare manoeuvre, and a directional 'kick' that was caused by local stall in the 'valley' of the inverted gull-wing in the three-point attitude. There were also complaints about forward visibility during the landing approach.

A request for proposal for a production F4U-1 Corsair was received by Vought from the Navy on 28 November 1940. By this time, the military requirements that had influenced the design of the XF4U-1 prototype had changed, and extensive modifications to the original design were required in order to improve the fighter's capabilities. The majority of these changes were directed toward increased fire power, heavier armour, increased protection for fuel and oil supplies, and higher power to meet demands for better performance. At the same time, other design changes were required to facilitate manufacturing and improve serviceability. Ease of mass production, unfortunately, had not influenced the

A side view comparison of the prototype XF4U-1 and the tenth production F4U-1 showing the only major change ever made to the Corsair's basic design; the aft relocation of the cockpit in order to provide space for the fuselage fuel tank./*US National Archives*

original 1938 Corsair design, because limited production runs in those days were normal and the threat of war was not yet considered to be great in America.

The four integral wing fuel tanks were eliminated in the F4U-1 and replaced with a single tank of the same capacity located in the fuselage directly aft of the engine firewall. This resulted in the only major change made to the Corsair's basic design. In order to provide space for the fuselage fuel tank, it was necessary to move the pilot and all related equipment aft 32 inches. Vision downward and aft over the trailing edge of the wing was improved, but vision downward and forward over the leading edge of the wing was somewhat reduced, further compounding the visibility problem during the landing approach. Vision forward over the engine cowl was unchanged, as the slope of the cowling was not modified. With the change from four wing tanks to one fuselage tank, the fuel system was greatly simplified, and it was felt that fuel feed would be much more positive.

The fuselage fuel tank could be bullet-proofed and had a capacity of 237 gallons, which included a standpipe reserve of 50 gallons. The two outer wing panel leading edge fuel tanks were retained in the F4U-1, and these tanks had a capacity of 63 gallons each. The outer panel tanks were equipped with a carbon dioxide vapour dilution system to provide protection against gunfire during combat by inerting the atmosphere above the fuel.

Armament was to consist of six machine guns. The two 30-calibre engine compartment guns were initially proposed to be retained in the F4U-1 with 500 rounds of ammunition per gun, and two 50-calibre guns were to be mounted in each outer wing panel adjacent to the centre section with 400 rounds of ammunition per gun. The 30-calibre engine compartment gun installation was eventually eliminated because of the requirement for heavier armament, and the airplane's final armament configuration was six 50-calibre machine guns, three mounted in each outer wing panel adjacent to the centre section. Six ammunition boxes in each outer panel supplied 400 rounds of ammunition to each inboard and intermediate gun, and 375 rounds to each outboard gun.

The bomb installation consisted of two Mark 41-2 bomb racks and two 100lb bombs, one mounted on each outer wing panel beneath the 50-calibre gun installations. Provisions for anti-aircraft bombs were eliminated, as were the wing-mounted flotation bags.

Aerodynamic modifications in the F4U-1 were directed at improving the airplane's stalling and low-speed stability characteristics. Aileron span was increased substantially to improve roll rate at the expense of reducing outboard flap span. The prototype's deflector plate flaps were replaced with NACA slotted flaps. A higher maximum lift coefficient was attainable with the slotted flaps, and also eliminated the requirement for deflector plates and gap closure operating mechanism that resulted in a less

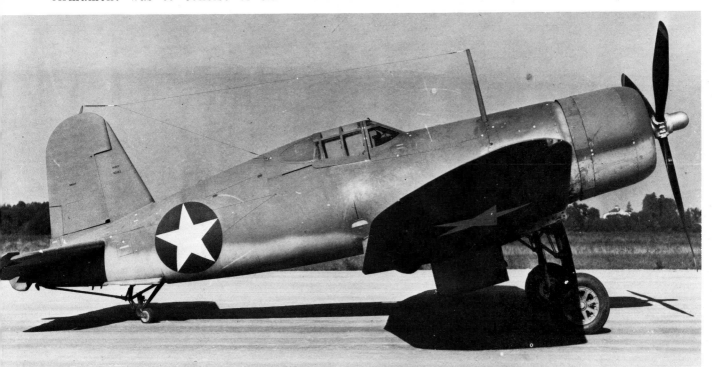

complicated and lighter weight flap system. Maximum flap deflection was decreased from 60 to 50 degrees to decrease drag in the landing configuration.

The XR-2800-4 engine used in the XF4U-1 was replaced in the F4U-1 with a Pratt & Whitney R-2800-8 'B' series Double Wasp engine. Armour protection was added around the cockpit and oil tank, and one and one-half inch thick laminated bullet-proof glass was installed behind the forward windshield. A jettisonable canopy was incorporated, and rearward vision was increased by adding cutouts and transparent panels aft of the pilot's headrest. Identification, friend or foe (IFF) radar transponder equipment was incorporated, and modifications were made to the arresting hook and tail landing gear systems. With regard to construction, a change was made to the use of a larger number of castings and forgings in the F4U-1.

Final Navy XF4U-1 demonstrations were completed by Boone Guyton at Anacostia Naval Air Station 24-25 February 1941. As a result of preliminary negotiations, a letter of intent for an F4U-1 production contract was received by Vought from the Navy on 3 March 1941. Vought submitted a proposal for the production F4U Corsair, designated VS-317, to the Navy on 2 April 1941, and on 30 June, received a formal contract for 584 airplanes, with initial deliveries scheduled to start in February, 1942.

On 1 November 1941, the Brewster Aeronautical Corporation was designated an associate contractor to supplement F4U-1 production (Brewster Corsairs were designated F3A-1). Brewster was eventually to build only 735 Corsairs before the badly managed company went out of business in July 1944. In December 1941, Goodyear Aircraft was also designated an associate F4U-1 contractor (Goodyear Corsairs were designated FG-1). Out of a total of 11,239 Corsairs built during World War II, Goodyear Aircraft built 3,941.

The Japanese attacked Pearl Harbour on 7 December 1941, and the F4U-1 was ordered into full-scale production. The first production F4U-1, Bureau of Aeronautics No 02153, made its maiden flight on 25 June 1942. The F4U-1s R-2800-8 engine produced 1,970hp at 2,700rpm at sea level, and 1,650hp at 2,700rpm at 23,000 feet. This high altitude power gave the F4U-1 a maximum speed of 397mph at 23,000feet. The plane had a sea level rate of climb of 3,000 feet per minute, and a service ceiling of 37,200 feet. Its gross weight in the combat condition was 12,061lbs.

The first production F4U-1 was delivered to the Navy on 31 July 1942, and while production and development work continued at Vought, the problem of adapting the Corsair to carrier operations had begun. The first carrier qualification trials for the airplane were held on 25 September 1942, aboard the escort carrier USS *Sangamon* in the Chesapeake Bay. The trials were performed by Lieutenant Commander Sam Porter in the seventh production Corsair, and four landings and

takeoffs were made. The results of the trials left the Navy with some serious doubts about the usefulness of the Corsair in the role of carrier fighter.

The relocation of the pilot well aft, together with the long round-nosed engine installation, combined to create a serious visibility problem on the early model F4U-1 in the nose-high three-point attitude. This problem was later alleviated by raising the pilot's seat seven inches, and redesigning the airplane's 'birdcage' canopy to a larger raised bubble type canopy, with a considerable improvement in vision. Oil from the hydraulically actuated cowl flaps and engine valve push rods spattered the windshield, compounding the visibility problem. This problem persisted until mechanical cowl flaps were installed, and the top section of the engine cowl was closed permanently.

The combination of a sharp break in

Above: A view from above of an early production version of the F4U-1. Except for successive canopy modifications, the F4U's outward appearance went virtually unchanged, the wing and tail areas remaining the same.
/US National Archives

Left: An early production version of the F4U-1 photographed in March 1943. The miniature bubble atop the front section of the 'Birdcage' canopy housed a rear view mirror.
/US National Archives

Centre left: One of the first production Brewster Aeronautical F3A-1 Corsairs. The Mark 41-2 bomb racks are visible under the leading edge of the outer wing panels.
/Brewster Aeronautical via William Larkins

Below left: The Corsair's main landing gear struts rotated through 87 degrees as they retracted aft to permit the wheels to lie flat in the wing where they were each completely enclosed by three doors.
/US National Archives

the airplane's lift curve scope near the stall, and the high power and torque of the propeller caused the Corsair to stall suddenly and drop its port wing unless a high level of pilot skill was used to hold it above the stall speed. Another peculiarity was the tendency of the airplane to bounce after touchdown. On initial contact with the carrier deck, the main landing gear oleos compressed, and then extended quickly back to full travel, bouncing the airplane back into the air. Yet another phenomenon was the 'rudder kick' which had been noted during XF4U-1 flight tests. All of these problems, while within the capability of many pilots, made it undesirable to operate the new fighter from a carrier deck, especially with newly-trained pilots.

The F4U-1s poor stalling characteristics were eventually alleviated by the addition of a small, six-inch long spoiler, or stall strip, that was mounted on the leading edge of the starboard outer wing panel just outboard of the gun ports. This small strip had the effect of spoiling the flow over the area of the wing immediately behind it. Since the port wing tended to stall first due to upwash from the propeller, the solution lay in forcing the starboard wing to stall at the same time. The 'rudder kick' problem was solved by increasing the length of the tail wheel strut. This reduced the Corsair's ground clearance angle from 13.5 to 11.5 degrees, thus reducing the percent of maximum lift coefficient used for landing, and the downwash angle over the tail. These improvements corrected almost all the early difficulties noted with the airplane. But meanwhile, it had gone into almost virtually exclusive ground based service with the US Marine Corps. The distinction of first introducing the Corsair to carrier duty was to go to the Royal Navy.

Below: A Corsair pilot takes the 'cut' from a Landing Signal Officer (LSO) during early carrier qualification trials.
/US National Archives

The Corsair Goes to War

With the war nearly ten months old, the first operating squadron to get Corsairs began accepting the new planes. Marine Fighter Squadron 124 (VMF-124) was formed on 7 September 1942, at Camp Kearney, California, and started receiving its Corsairs toward the end of that same month. VMF-124 was destined to be the first squadron to take Corsairs into combat, and was commanded by Major William E. Gise.

While the men and planes of VMF-124 were being groomed for combat, Marine pilots on Guadalcanal were putting up a one-sided, but remarkably effective battle against superior Japanese air power. Flying Grumman F4F Wildcats from Henderson Field, fighter pilots were running up high scores against the Japanese pilots. Despite the fact that the Zero could out-perform the F4F in almost

every respect, superior tactics were beginning to have their effect upon superior Japanese planes. By the time the Corsairs were to arrive in the South Pacific, Japanese airpower over the Solomons, if not already wrecked, was certainly reeling. US losses had been heavy, however, and increasingly better Japanese fighters were soon to reach the South Pacific. The Corsair would have its job cut out for it.

The twenty-two F4U-1s of VMF-124 were declared combat ready on 28 December, by which time a total of 178 Corsairs had rolled off the assembly lines.

On 12 February 1943, the first Corsair equipped Marine fighter squadron went into action in the South Pacific. Twelve Corsairs of VMF-124 were flown up to Guadalcanal in the morning from Espiritu Santo, and escorted a group of

Navy PBY Catalinas on a rescue mission that afternoon. Altogether these pilots logged nine hours in their F4Us that first day in action, a good indication of the extent to which the Marines would employ their new plane. On their second day in action, the F4Us escorted Navy PB4Y Liberators on a 300-mile bombing mission to Bougainville and return, a mission previously out of the question for Marine F4F Wildcat fighters.

On 14 February, while flying fighter escort on an attack mission to Kahili Field in southern Bougainville, the Marine F4U pilots learned that the Japanese flyers had not lost their skill or aggressiveness. About 50 well-alerted Zeros were waiting for the raid and in the melee that followed, the Japanese shot down two F4Us, two Navy PB4Y Liberators, two Army P-40 Warhawks, and the entire top cover of four Army P-38 Lightnings, with a loss to themselves of only three Zeros, one of which collided with an F4U.

It wasn't long after this 'Saint Valentine's Day Massacre' that the F4Us gained an aerial superiority over the Japanese fighters which they never relinquished. Japanese officers interrogated after the war said that they considered the Corsair the best fighter the US had in the Pacific.

During its combat tour in the

Below: A USMC Corsair settles on to the runway on Vella Lavella Island, in the New Georgia Group, after completing a mission against the Japanese, 15 December 1943.
/US National Archives

Top right: A USMC Corsair being refuelled at Munda, on New Georgia Island, August 1943.
/US National Archives

Bottom right: A lonely vigil; a guard protects newly constructed Corsairs in the rain.
/US National Archives

Solomons, VMF-124 claimed 68 enemy planes against a combat loss of 11 planes and three pilots. Meanwhile, Marine fighter squadrons were being rapidly equipped with the Corsair and by 2 July 1943, there were eight squadrons operating Corsairs in the South Pacific.

The first Corsair ace, Lieutenant Kenneth A. Walsh of VMF-124, wasn't long in establishing his mark. On 1 April 1943, the Japanese sent 58 Zeros sweeping down the Solomons, and in that melee, Walsh got three. On 13 May 1943, a group of Army and Marine fighters ran into 25 Zeros over Guadalcanal. Walsh got three more, running his score up to six, one more than he needed to become an ace. (He wound up eventually with 21.) Major Gise, the CO of VMF-124, was killed in the fight in which Walsh became an ace.

As the fighting moved up the Solomons, Corsairs spearheaded the advance and, in the process, gained increasing favour. Lieutenant Wilbur Thomas of VMF-213, while shooting down four enemy planes over Rendova, is said to have reported that his Corsair 'performed wonderfully.' Major Gregory Weissenberger, CO of VMF-213, in the same flight, shot down three Zekes in 60 seconds with his Corsair. Lieutenant Walsh, leading a division of five Corsairs during the landings on Vella Lavella, got into a fight after being jumped by five Zekes at 10,000 feet. He chased one Zeke for five miles, and then shot it down. Turning, he ran into nine Vals, come up under them and shot two down. Sandwiched between Vals below and Zekes above, he got two 20-millimetre holes in his right wing, a hydraulic line was cut, his horizontal stabiliser was punctured, and his right tyre blown.

Walsh was cheered when he landed back at Munda, but his airplane was so badly damaged it had to be junked. That was one in countless instances in which the ability of the Corsair to take punishment was to be thoroughly proven.

Fifteen days later, Walsh had engine trouble, landed his Corsair at Munda, and got another. He then rejoined his group at Kahili and shot down four enemy fighters during a lone battle with what he reported as approximately 50 of them. Again he was shot up, but this time too badly to get back to dry land, and he was forced to make a dead-stick landing off Vella Lavella.

On 28 August, another Corsair pilot, Lieutenant Alvin J. Jensen of VMF-214, performed one of the great single-handed feats of the Pacific War during a sweep of Kahili. Separated in a tropical storm from the rest of his flight, Jensen came out of it upside down, right over the Japanese field. He rolled his plane over at the north end of the field and started

Above: USMC Corsairs taxi out to the Turtle Bay Fighter Strip on Espiritu Santo, in the New Hebrides Group, 5 October 1943./*US National Archives*

Right: USMC Corsairs prepare to takeoff from the Barakoma Fighter Strip on Vella Lavella Island./*US Navy via Jim Sullivan*

Below right: A USMC pilot leaves his Corsair parked by the runway at Munda, on New Georgia Island, August 1943. /*US National Archives*

Far right, top: A USMC ground crewman boresighting a Corsair's six 50-calibre machine guns on Bougainville, in the Solomon Islands, February, 1944. /*US National Archives*

Far right, bottom: Members of an F4U-1's ground crew hoist the tail of the Corsair in preparation for boresighting and test firing the plane's machine guns on Bougainville, February 1944. /*US National Archives*

strafing the aircraft lined up along the runway. Flying only a few feet above the ground, he destroyed eight Zekes, four Vals, and twelve Bettys before streaking for home. Photographs taken the next day confirmed his claim of destroying 24 enemy aircraft on the ground.

Meanwhile, during combat practice in early January 1943, a captured Japanese Zero had been put up against an F4U-1. The Corsair proved itself definitely superior. Also, in combat practice with a P-51 Mustang, the Corsair consistently outfought its 'opponent' above 12,000 feet and was considered evenly matched below that altitude. The F4U-1 also played an important part in the Eglin Air Base, Florida, Fighter Evaluation Meet, which started on 21 May 1943. Army pilots, flying the Corsair for the first time, were enthusiastic in their praise of the fighter. Dogfights were held with the P-47 Thunderbolt, P-51 Mustang, P-38 Lightning, and P-39 Airacobra Army fighters, all with favourable results.

Right: A mechanic checking his Corsair's cowl on Bougainville, February 1944.
/US National Archives

Below: USMC armourers aligning and adjusting a Corsair's port battery of three 50-calibre machine guns prior to boresighting and harmonisation on Bougainville, February 1944.
/US National Archives

Above: A USMC Corsair being refuelled after a mission at Munda, August 1943.
/*US National Archives*

Right: A USMC pilot landing his Corsair on the Torokina Airstrip at Empress Augusta Bay, Bougainville, 10 January 1944. The pilot is hunched over the controls and looking out the side of the cockpit for reference because of the poor forward visibility in the landing approach attitude. One of the US Army P-39 Airacobras that shared the field with the Marines is visible in the background.
/*USMC via Rowland Gill*

Below right: Against a background of shell-shattered coconut palms, a USMC Corsair taxis down the muddy runway at Munda, 26 August 1943. VMF-123 'Eight-Ball' and VMF-124 'Checkerboard' Corsairs began operating from the airstrip nine days after it was captured on 5 August 1943.
/*USMC via Rowland Gill*

Top left: A USMC Corsair taxiing along the runway at Munda, August 1943.
/*US National Archives*

Centre left: A USMC Corsair lifting off the Torokina Airstrip at Empress Augusta Bay on Bougainville, 16 December 1943./*US National Archives*

Below: A USMC Corsair, piloted by Major Robert G. Owens, the CO of VMF-215, the 'Fighting Corsairs', gets a tow after being bogged down in the mud off the edge of the runway on Munda, August 1943.
/*US National Archives*

Right: A 'Birdcage' canopy USMC Corsair passes some of the newer raised canopy versions as it taxis down the coral taxiway on Espirito Santo, 8 March 1944.
/*USMC via Rowland Gill*

Below right: Royal New Zealand Air Force P-40 Warhawks and USMC Corsairs on Espiritu Santo, March 1944.
/*US National Archives*

Black Sheep
Colonel Gregory 'Pappy' Boyington, USMC (Ret.)

'Pappy' Boyington, then a Major, took command of VMF-214 at Munda on 7 September 1943. He describes how VMF-214 got its squadron name, the Black Sheep, and then, the first combat mission the squadron flew under his command:

"We were loaned the number 214 from another squadron that had just completed a combat tour, but a name was needed for our squadron. The majority of the squadrons' names had something to do with women, but these pilots had the idea that we had been deprived of some of the things other squadrons enjoyed, so they agreed upon Boyington's Bastards and seemed pleased with the name."

But later, Boyington had to tell the squadron —

'We are going to have to choose a squadron name that is fit to print, my friends.'

'Just what do you mean, Gramps?'

'I mean Boyington's Bastards. In the first place, I don't think a squadron should be named after a person. And in the second place, a correspondent said last night they would balk at printing it back home.'

'There was a great hassle following this, and some of the many suggestions followed: "Outcasts?" "Forgotten Freddies?" "Bold Bums?"'

'To hell with 'em, we'll do such a job they'll have to print it and like it.' So it appeared we were right back where we had started.

'No, Gramps. We have thought it over, suggested names, but we like the one we already have. Besides, we have been treated like bastards, and our name rhymes.'

"I had an answer, but I didn't tell the boys where it came from for fear they would laugh me out of the ready shack.

"Since my childhood, the noises made by trains and motors of various types had played a little jingle with my thinking upon many an occasion. My recollection of these occasions when I had been

Below: Major Gregory 'Pappy' Boyington's 'Black Sheep' Squadron, VMF-214 on Espiritu Santo. Boyington is wearing a baseball cap and is in the centre of the front row kneeling beneath the Corsair's propeller hub, 11 September 1943.
/US National Archives

Above: VMF-124 'Black Sheep' pilots scramble to their Corsairs on Espiritu Santo, in the New Hebrides Group, 11 September 1943. L to R: Major Gregory Boyington, Lieutenant Roland N. Rinabarger, Captain Robert T. Ewing and Lieutenant Henry M. Bourgeois./*US National Archives*

Left: A division of four VMF-214 'Black Sheep' Corsairs over Bougainville, in the Solomon Islands, February 1944.
/*US National Archives*

33

pleasantly occupied with daydreams was most enjoyable. My childhood jingle was, 'Baa Baa Blacksheep, have you any wool, yes sir, yes sir, three bags full.'

"So I said: 'Say fellows, I got an idea! Something we could use in polite society. Something society already accepts.'

'Okay spill it, Gramps.'

'Try this for size. Black Sheep. Everybody knows that it stands for the same thing. And yet no personality is involved, and they can print Black Sheep.'

'By golly, we like that, Gramps. We can make a bastard coat of arms like they used to do in England, and we can put it on a shield and use it as our insignia.'

"Several days passed before the boys obtained all the authentic dope they needed for drawing up the shield, or insignia. Someone explained that the bar on a bastard shield ran diagonally in the opposite direction from the legitimate. So we made ours this way. They also decided a black sheep was to be on the shield . . ."

"The afternoon of our arrival in the Russell Islands, I was called by Strike Command. Our first mission was scheduled for a 7.00am takeoff the following morning, 16 September 1943. I had little sleep that night. For tomorrow, I imagined the ghouls would be watching

Right: A USMC Corsair taxiing out for a mission at an unknown South Pacific location. /*US National Archives*

Below: A USMC Corsair over Espiritu Santo, March 1944. /*US National Archives*

and hoping to see the poor little ole squadron flub its duff.

"No one, I believe, noticed how concerned I was. Probably this escaped the officers in Strike Command, because I did nothing more than smoke one cigarette after another. This was not unusual . . ."

"It was a temporary relief to get the hell out of the briefing shack and away from the officers in Strike Command. 'Moon' was waiting patiently in one of the jeeps to drive Stan, myself, and a couple of others down to the end of the strip, where our mighty Corsairs awaited like sleek, silent steeds. Truly a picture of beauty, in my opinion, were these new ships, the Corsairs.

"Twenty Corsairs — five flights of four from our squadron — and of course twenty pilots were to escort three squadrons of Dauntless dive bombers and two squadrons of Avenger torpedo planes, totalling 150 bombers in all.

"The mission was to wipe out Ballale. A small island west of Bougainville, heavily fortified, and all airfield, not unlike La Guardia. The main difference was that we knew the traffic was going to be much more congested than the New York area is today, without the aid of Air Traffic Control directing our flight

patterns. Besides the lack of ATC, as we know and depend upon it now, our traffic would be further distorted by anti-aircraft fire, and God only knows how many Zeros.

"And again, I don't believe that I gave a second thought to the fact that we had to fly six hundred miles round trip as the crows fly, up and down the old 'slot', sparsely dotted with tiny islands, most of these islands being Japanese held. The main worry was whether our seams would hold together as a squadron.

"Our first problem was to get 170 aircraft off a single strip closely enough together, in time, that is, so that we would have adequate fuel to complete the trip yet leave ourselves a half hour's more fuel for a fight at full throttle. A P&W 2,000hp engine at full throttle used the old petrol much the same as if it were going through a floodgate.

"Wandering around our aircraft, getting a nod, or seeing a wave that each one after the other was in readiness, calmed me down rapidly. Soon we received the start-up-engine signal. One by one the shotgun starters audibly fired out black smoke. Each engine would go into a few convulsive coughs, afterwards smoothing out into a steady roar. Everything seemed much smoother, smooth as the perfect Venturi form of water vapour formed in misty silhouette about each ship, caused by the propeller and the extremely high humidity of the island air.

"Takeoff time — the last Dauntless had wobbled lazily into the air, starting to turn in one gigantic join-up circle. We took off in pairs down the snowy white coral strip at about twenty-second intervals, which was a feat in itself, because none of us had more than approximately thirty hours in these powerful new speed birds.

"As we climbed, in shorter radii than the bombers, we gradually came abreast of the bomber leader, pulling up above and behind him. Radio silence was in effect. We had no intention of broadcasting our departure to the Japanese. The squadron was spread out like a loose umbrella over the bombers by use of hand signals. A reminder to lean out and reduce prop rpm was passed along to all hands in order to conserve precious fuel.

"We settled down to the monotony of flying herd on the bombers. Our huge paddle-blade propellers were turning so slowly it seemed as if I counted each blade as it passed by. Hour after hour, it felt. The magnetism of counting those

36

blades was so great I was tempted on several occasions to blurt out over the radio: 'Who could ever believe this damn ocean could be so damn big!'

"The group commander, leading the bombers, was responsible for the navigation. I didn't have that worry. Finally, the monotony was to be broken up, because we were flying above fleecy layers of stratus that demanded all my concentration to hold the shadowy forms of the bombers below in sight. Actually, the reason we had this cloud separation was that the bombers had to fly between stratus layers too. There wasn't enough space for us to fly in the visual part of the sandwich and still remain above the bombers.

"Thoughts of how we might louse up the all-important rendezvous after takeoff were far behind. We had made that. And the rendezvous ahead, after our mission was accomplished, certainly couldn't have bothered me. For the Brass couldn't possibly see that, only the Nips could. And I don't believe I gave too much thought to them.

"A new worry took its place. The clouds being the way they were, no Nip planes could find us. No action. The high command would undoubtedly have us all back as replacement pilots . . ."

"Hardly had I gotten through feeling sorry for myself when I noticed the dive bombers had all disappeared from sight . . ." "I lowered the squadron through a thin layer of stratus to try to find the bomber boys. Upon breaking clear, the noise from my earphones almost broke my eardrums. One thing was for darn sure. There was no more radio silence in effect. After a few sensible words like: 'Stop being nervous. Talk slower.' Words came back more shrilly and faster: 'Who's nervous? You son-of-a-bitch, not me-ee.' Then communications settled down to a garbled roar.

"Avengers and Dauntlesses, which appeared to be streaking downward in dives at all angles, were making rack and ruin upon what, I realized suddenly, was Ballale. Some had already pulled out of their dives. Others were just in the process of pulling out. And still others were in their dives.

"Huge puffs of dirt and smoke started to dot the tiny isle. A white parachute mushroomed out amid the dirty grayish puffs. Of course I realised it was at a higher altitude. Then a place crashed. Avenger or Dauntless? How was I to know.

"There were enough thick clouds over nearby Bourgainville so that I did not expect any Jap Zeros to intercept us from there. I don't know what I was thinking right at that particular moment. Or what I was supposed to be doing. Maybe, as the proverbial saying goes: 'I sat there fat, dumb, and happy'. Perhaps I was watching the boys below in much the same manner as I witnessed the Cleveland Air shows many times. Anyhow, for certain, high cover was about as close as I ever expected to get toward Heaven. So we started down.

"To add to my bewilderment, shortly after we cleared the last bit of fluff, I saw that we were right in the middle of about forty Jap fighters. As for us, we had twenty planes that day.

"The first thing I knew, there was a Japanese fighter plane, not more than twenty-five feet off my right wing tip. Wow, the only marking I was conscious of was the 'Angry Red Meat Ball' sailing alongside of me. But I guess the Nip pilot never realised what I was, because he wobbled his wings, which, in pilot language means join up. Then he added throttle, pulling ahead of my Corsair.

"Good God! It had all happened so suddenly, I hadn't turned on my gun switches, electric gun sight, or, for that matter, even charged my machine guns. All of which is quite necessary if one desires to shoot someone down in the air.

"It seemed like an eternity before I could get everything turned on and the guns charged. But when I did accomplish all this, I joined up on the Jap, all right. He went spiralling down in flames right off Ballale.

"The bursts from my six 50-calibre machine guns, the noise and seeing tracer bullets, brought me back to this world once again. Like someone had hit me with a wet towel. Almost simultaneously I glanced back over my shoulder to see how Moe Fisher, my wingman, was making out and because I saw tracers go sizzling past my right wing tip. Good boy, Moe — he was busy pouring an endless burst into a Nip fighter, not more than fifty yards off the end of my tail section. This Nip burst into flames as he started to roll, minus half a wing, towards the sea below.

"In these few split seconds all concern, and, for that matter, all view of the dive

bombers, left me again. All that stood out in my vision were burning and smoking aircraft. And all I could make out were Japanese having this trouble. Some were making out-of-control gyrations toward a watery grave ..."

"After a few seconds of Fourth-of-July spectacle most of the Nip fighters cleared out. Then we streaked on down lower to the water, where the dive bombers were re-forming for mutual protection after their dives prior to proceeding homeward. We found a number of Nip fighters making runs on our bombers while they were busy re-forming their squadrons.

"While travelling at quite an excessive rate of speed for making an approach on one of these Zeros I opened fire on his cockpit, expecting him to turn either right or left, or go up or down to evade my fire after he was struck by my burst. But this Zero didn't do any of these things. It exploded. It exploded so close, right in front of my face, that I didn't know which way to turn to miss the pieces. So I flew right through the centre of the explosion, throwing up my arm in front of my face in a feeble attempt to ward off these pieces.

"I didn't know what happened to my plane at the time. Evidently, my craft didn't hit the Nip's engine when his plane flew apart. But I did have dents all over my engine cowling and leading edges of my wings and empennage surfaces. With this unorthodox evasive action Moe and I were finally separated as by this time, I guessed, everyone else was. Certainly this wasn't the procedure we followed in the three-week training period ..."

"Long after the bombing formation had gone on toward home, I found a Zero scooting along, hugging the water, returning to his base after chasing our bombers as far as he thought wise. This I had gotten from the past. When an aircraft is out of ammunition or low on fuel, the pilot will hug the terrain in order to present a very poor target.

"I decided to make a run on this baby. He never changed his course much, but started an ever-so-gentle turn. My Corsair gradually closed the gap between us. I was thinking: 'As long as he is turning, he knows he isn't safe. It looks too easy'.

"Then I happened to recall something I had experienced in Burma with the Flying Tigers, so I violently reversed my course. And sure enough, there was his little pal coming along behind me. He was just waiting for the sucker, me, to commence my pass on his mate.

"As I turned into his pal, I made a head-on run with him. Black puffs came slowly from his 20-millimetre cannons. His tracers were dropping way under my Corsair. I could see my tracers going all around his little Zero. When I got close enough to him, I could see rips in the bottom of his fuselage as I ducked underneath on my pass by. The little plane nosed down slowly, smoking, and crashed with a splash a couple of seconds later, without burning or flaming.

"Efforts to locate the other Zero, the intention of my initial run, proved to be futile. In turning east again, in the direction of our long-gone bombers, once more I happened on a Zero barrelling homeward just off the water. This time there was no companion opponent with the plane. So I nosed over, right off the

Top left: A USMC Corsair parked along the beach on Majuro Atoll, in the Marshall Islands, August 1944./*US National Archives*

Bottom left: USMC Corsairs parked along the runway on Enigebi Island, August 1944./*US National Archives*

Below: USMC Corsairs taxi by Marine Night Fighter Squadron VMF (N)-534 F6F-5N Hellcats at the Orote Peninsula Airstrip on Guam, in the Mariana Islands, 20 August 1944. /*USMC via Rowland Gill*

water and made a head-on run from above on this Japanese fighter. I wondered whether the pilot didn't see me or was so low on fuel he didn't dare to change his direction for home.

"A short burst of 50s, then smoke. While I was endeavouring to make a turn to give the coup de grace, the plane landed in the ocean. When the aircraft hit the water going at any speed like that, they don't remain on the surface. They hit like a rock and sink out of sight immediately. For the first time I became conscious that I would never have enough fuel to get back to home base in the Russell Islands, but I could make it to Munda, New Georgia. Ammunition — well, I figured that must be gone. Lord knows, the trigger had been held down long enough. Anyhow there would be no need for more ammo.

"But the day still wasn't ended, even though this recital of the first day's events may start seeming a little repetitious by now. And God knows, I was certainly through for the day, in more ways than one. Yet when practically back to our closest allied territory, which was then Munda, I saw one of our Corsairs proceeding for home along the water. I tried to join up with him.

"And just then, as if from nowhere, I saw that two Nip fighters were making runs on this Corsair at their leisure. The poor Corsair was so low it couldn't dive or make a turn in either direction if he wanted to, with two on this tail. There was oil all over the plexiglass canopy and sides of the fuselage. Undoubtedly, his speed had to be reduced in order to nurse the injured engine as far as possible.

"In any event, if help didn't arrive quickly, the pilot, whoever he was, would be a goner soon. I made a run from behind on the Zero closer to the Corsair. This Zero pulled straight up — for they can really manoeuvre — almost straight up in the air. I was hauling back on my stick so hard that my plane lost speed and began to fall into a spin. And as I started to spin, I saw the Zero break into flames. A spin at that low altitude is a pretty hairy thing in itself, and I no doubt would have been more concerned if so many other things weren't happening at the same time.

"It was impossible for me to see this flamer crash. By this time, I was too occupied getting my plane out of the spin before I hit the water too. I did, however, shoot a sizable burst into the second Zero a few seconds later. This Zero turned northward for Choiseul, a nearby enemy-held island, but without an airstrip. The only thing I could figure was that his craft

was acting up and he planned upon ditching as close to Choiseul as he could. Anyhow, I didn't have sufficient gas to verify my suspicions.

"Also, I was unable to locate the oil-smeared Corsair again. Not that it would have helped any, or there was anything else one could do, but I believe Bod Ewing must have been in that Corsair. For Bob never showed up after the mission. And one thing for certain, that slowed-down, oil smeared, and shell-ridden Corsair couldn't have gone much farther.

"This first day of the new squadron had been a busy one, all right. It had been so busy I suddenly realised my gas gauge was bouncing on empty. And I wanted so badly to stretch that gas registering zero to somewhere close to Munda I could taste it.

"I leaned out fuel consumption as far as was possible, and the finish was one of those photo ones. I did reach the field at Munda, or rather one end of it, and was just starting to taxi down the field when my engine cut out. I was completely out of gas.

"The armourers came out to rearm my plane and informed me that I had only thirty rounds of 50-calibre left, so I guess I did come back at the right time.

"But I was to learn something else, too, in case I started to think that all my days were to be like this one, the first one. For this first day — when I got five planes to my credit — happened to be the best day I ever had in combat."

'Pappy' Boyington and his Black Sheep Squadron developed the technique of the fighter sweep at Rabaul. The first sweep was made on 17 December 1943, with Boyington leading 31 F4Us, 23 P-40 Warhawks and 22 F6F Hellcats. Boyington radioed pleas to the Japanese to come up and fight, but few rose to meet the challenge. After that unsuccessful flight, Boyington argued that 76 planes were too many. On the next sweep he took 48, mostly Corsairs, and they shot down 30 Japanese fighters. (Boyington ran his personal score from 20 to 24, including six he had shot down in China while he was serving with the Flying Tigers.) In subsequent raids, Corsair-led fighter sweeps destroyed Japanese airpower over Rabaul.

On 3 January 1944, Boyington was shot down, together with his wingman, Captain George M. Ashmun. Other squadron pilots reported that they had seen Boyington shoot down one plane before he went down, bringing his personal score to 26 planes. Boyington parachuted into St George's Channel when his flaming Corsair had only 200 or 300 feet of altitude left. Four Zekes strafed him for 15 or 20 minutes, but never hit him. Just before dark, a Japanese submarine surfaced and took him prisoner. After six weeks on Rabaul, he was put on board a transport plane and then taken to Truk. Eventually, the Japanese carried their No 1 aviator prisoner to Japan, where he was interned

Top left: USMC Corsairs parked on Majuro Atoll, August 1944./*US National Archives*

Centre left: A USMC Corsair landing on the Barakoma Fighter Strip on Vella Lavella Island, 20 January 1944. /*US National Archives*

Bottom left: Ground crewmen preparing a USMC Corsair for a mission on Espiritu Santo, March 1944./*US National Archives*

Below: USMC Corsairs in flight over ships anchored off Eniwetok Atoll, in the Marshall Islands, 9 July 1944. /*US National Archives*

until the end of the war. After the war, Boyington described how he had shot down two additional planes on his last flight, bringing his total score to 28, making him the US Marine Corps' highest scoring ace in World War II.

Thirty-three years after he was shot down, 'Pappy' had this to say to the author about the Corsair —

"Actually, Dick, I loved the Corsair. It was one of the most welcome sights to come along at that particular time. Now, we were flying the Grumman F4F Wildcat in the early part of the war out there in the southwest Pacific, and it was a good little plane. But, the Japanese Zero was faster and could outclimb us, and all the Japanese planes could out-turn us. The F4F was a durable little piece of equipment, but you had to have a partner to protect your blind side, and if you got in a fight, you would have to stay there and fight until the Japanese either got short on gas, or ran out of ammo and decided to let you go home. And this is not the most comfortable situation to be in. But with the advent of the Corsair, we could finally outclimb the Japanese, and we also had more speed. We could close on them and didn't have to wait for them to close on us. In other words, we were taking over the advantage; we were the aggressor for a change. Of course, we couldn't out-turn them, but what we could do was: say I was going in and trying to get a shot, and the man avoiding me goes into a turn. Now, he plans on eventually working around to getting on my tail because he can turn tighter than I can, but if I couldn't get him in my sight with the proper deflection lead — in say a half a turn — and I see him working around, then I would just merely climb, and then come down and make another half turn with him. And, depending upon how much time and gas I had, and how good a shot I was, it was only a matter of time until he would run away, or I would shoot him down. So, the Corsair was a very welcome sight. Now, the same identical R-2800 engine that was in the Corsair was also in the Navy F6F. Yet, at an altitude of, say, 20,000ft, where we would fly over enemy territory because we didn't want those people above us, the F6F was about 10 to 20 knots slower than the Corsair. Well, this didn't seem to mean a lot when we were going close to 400 knots. However, that little bit makes one heck of a lot of difference in many cases. And I think the proof of this is that more F6Fs got shot down than Corsairs — just with that small amount of margin. Another little bit of margin was that the Corsair could turn just a little better than the F6F. Now, I'm not trying to run down a Grumman product and build up a Chance Vought product, because I've

flown both people's planes and they're both wonderful companies.

"With all its advantages, it also had — as with everything else that's good — something that wasn't so good about it. The Corsair had a long nose and when it was in the three-point position, taxying or landing, you were almost completely blind looking forward. Of course, you never experienced this in combat or in actual flight. But, in your landing and in your taxying, and during takeoff before you got your tail up, you couldn't look out the front, which you customarily would do in all the other planes you'd flown previously. The runways out there were, for the most part, very narrow, so I know what I did, and what I instructed my pilots to do: 'Do not try to fly it like another airplane or taxi it like another airplane — look straight out the side. Kick your plane around at the end of the runway and you look down the runway to see if it's clear, and then kick it back around and just look out the side at 90 degrees until you get your tail up, and then you can look out the front. The same is true for landing. Once you get in a three-point position, put your eye out 90 degrees. If it wasn't clear the last time you saw it, that runway will never be clear, that's one little chance you're going to have to take.'

"I know that the Corsair was originally designed and ordered in great numbers for the United States Navy. But, when Navy pilots first landed them on a carrier, they were horrified! The planes were hanging on the prop when they were in the carrier pattern, and at the point when they got directly behind the carrier for a long period, they were nose-high, even higher than for a three-point landing. And these guys said, 'We don't want this!' And I guess they banged up their share of airplanes during those first carrier landings. Anyhow, they then asked themselves — 'What'll we do? This big order, and all this money is spent.' That's quite simple if you're one of the high command in the Navy. You do it this way. 'We'll give them to the Marine Corps.' The Navy, for the most part, is very kind to the Marine Corps, but every once in awhile, they use them as garbage cans, just because they're convenient. If there was anything else more convenient, they'd probably use it, and no sour grapes; I mean, this was just human nature. The Marines got the Corsairs, and they were all working off land bases. Of course, we really showed the Navy how to use the Corsair. In fact, we showed everybody concerned, including the enemy, how to do that. Now the first people to land on the carriers, Marines when we finally got to that point — were so familiar with that plane that this long nose and the blind spot didn't bother them like it would somebody just going in for the first few times. I mean, this was just all-geared into them by that time."

Skull and Crossbones
Captain John T. 'Tommy' Blackburn, USN (Ret.)

Right: VF-17's insignia, a Jolly Roger 'Skull and Crossbones' pirate flag./*US National Archives*

Below: One of VF-17's 'Birdcage' canopy F4U-1s on the USS *Bunker Hill* (CVE 17) during her shakedown cruise in the Caribbean Sea, 5 July 1943. /*US National Archives*

Far right, top: A prelude to blown main gear tyres; one of VF-17s F4U-1s is about to be snapped down on the deck of the USS *Bunker Hill* (CVE-17), 7 July 1943./*US National Archives*

Far right, bottom: This VF-17 F4U-1 was piloted by Ensign Ferguson who had just made the 1,000th landing aboard the USS *Bunker Hill* (CVE-17), 28 July 1944./*US National Archives*

Navy Fighter Squadron 17 (VF-17), under the command of Lieutenant Commander John T. 'Tommy' Blackburn, was formed on 1 January 1943. VF-17 was to become the first US Navy squadron to see action with Corsairs. The squadron was attached to the USS *Bunker Hill*, but became a land-based fighter unit after arriving in the New Georgia area in September 1943. Blackburn's Skull and Crossbones Squadron was the first to be equipped with the new raised canopy F4U-1s.

Called the 'greatest Navy fighter squadron in history', VF-17 and its Corsairs shot down 127 Japanese aircraft in 75 days of combat. (In one five-day period they shot down 60.) Fifteen aces, more than in any other Pacific fighter unit, were credited to VF-17. One of them, Lieutenant Ira C. 'Ike' Kepford,

was the Navy's leading ace at that time, with 16 kills. On 11 November 1943, during one of the carrier strikes on Rabaul, the land-based Corsairs of VF-17 provided high cover for the carriers USS *Essex*, USS *Bunker Hill* and USS *Independence*. In the course of protecting the carriers, the fact that the Corsair could be deck-landed by experienced pilots was demonstrated when the VF-17 Corsairs landed aboard the carriers to refuel and rearm, becoming the first US Navy F4Us to operate from a carrier in combat.

Here now is the story of VF-17, the Skull and Crossbones Squadron, as told by its CO, Captain John T. 'Tommy' Blackburn, USN (Ret.).

"Clear, moonless night, 24 Corsair fighters in three loose formations of eight showing only dim blue formation lights on top of their wingtips, some small amount of orange flame from the exhaust manifolds, dim red lighting in the cockpits, 170 miles out over the Solomons Sea. Where the hell is the Fast Carrier Task Force? No joy on the Hayrake! (No signal via the radio homing device on the USS *Bunker Hill*.) Suddenly the radio silence is broken: 'Big Hog (me) this is Chuck (Pillsbury). Judah (USS *Essex*) Hayrake loud and clear, Channel 7.'

"We home in on the signal and go into a

One of VF-17s F4U-1s about to touchdown on the deck of the USS *Charger* (ACV-30) in Chesapeake Bay during the squadron's initial carrier landing qualifications, 8 March 1943. /*US Navy Archives*

wide circular holding pattern at 10,000 feet, well aware that we have been tracked in by the ships' radars, aware too, that the radio transmission has been heard so that there is no need to make a report 'on station', which may serve to alert the Japs that there is trouble brewing for them. When daylight breaks and we can be useful, the Task Force fighter director will open up, station us where he thinks we will be most effective, or vector us out to intercept snoopers or incoming raids.

"With the dawn we can see the USS *Bunker Hill*, the USS *Essex*, and the USS *Independence* with their nine screening destroyers leaving white swaths in the dark blue as they knife into the wind at 25 knots launching planes for the upcoming strike on Rabaul. We're there along with 12 Hellcats from Monk Russell's squadron shorebased at Segi to provide fighter cover for the Task Force so that all the carrier's planes can be used.

"This is a unique operation in that two Navy squadrons have the equipment and the know-how to fly out from 'the beach', to work with the ships, to land aboard, to refuel and re-arm, and then to be launched to get back to work and eventually return to our shore bases. 11 November 1943 turns out to be quite a day.

" 'Big Hog this is Judah — Bogey! Angels 15 — vector 350 — buster!' (Probable enemy plane at 15,000 feet, steer 350 degrees at full speed.) 'This is Big Hog — wilco.' Shortly, 'Tally-ho'. A lone Jap fighter, an Army Tony below, heads toward the carriers. He sees us coming and desperately dives for the cover of a cumulus cloud. I manage to get there in time (just ahead of Kepford) and flame him. 'Judah this is Big Hog — splash one Tony — returning to station.'

"There is no further enemy activity as the Strike Group forms up and disappears to the north. Suddenly, 'Big Hog — your signal is Charlie.' So I lead 12 Corsairs to land aboard the USS *Bunker Hill*; Roger Hedrick takes 12 to the USS *Essex*, and John Kelly goes with his Hellcats on to the USS *Independence*. A very professional performance, as the carrier skippers are quick to remark: no missed

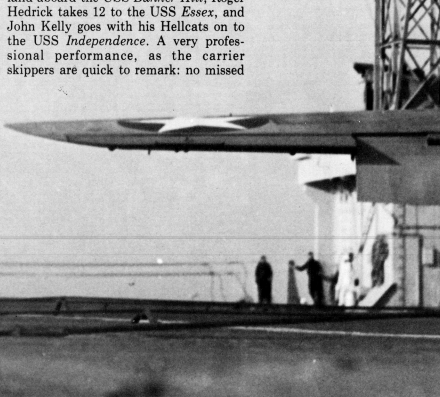

approaches, good tight landing intervals, no thrillers and none of us has so much as seen a carrier for three months.

"It's old home week aboard the *Bunker Hill*, our ship during training and shakedown, and we're made to feel more than welcome. I charge up to the bridge to be fondly greeted by that superb skipper, Captain John Ballentine. I point out the two Jap flags on my plane and collect $10 from the Air Boss, Kit Carson, who has bet me that the ship will see action before VF-17 does. (We had left the ship at Pearl Harbour in September.) So down to the wardroom for fresh orange juice, honest-to-God scrambled eggs and bacon, complete with linen tablecloth and napkins. What a change from the battery acid, spam and powdered eggs provided by the scruffy chow hall at the Hotel Mud Plaza at Ondonga!

"Back in the air again, to be comfortably established at various altitudes over the Task Force before the Strike Group returns, ready to counter the Jap forces that are expected to follow in its wake.

"The Strike Group gets back about 1300, and the carriers swing smartly into the wind for the landing aboard. Cripples and low states (those short on fuel) land first.

"Sure enough, many bogies closing from the North. By this time the usual heavy cumulo-nimbus clouds have formed and the incoming enemy is skilfully using the thunderheads for visual cover and to confuse the ship's radars.

"What happens for the following half hour can be described as chaotic — a wild melee of anti-aircraft (AA) fire, burning planes splashing, bomb geysers, ships twisting and turning at maximum speeds to dodge bombs and torpedoes, voice

Above: Deck crewmen stand by as one of the VF-17's F4U-1s is about to touchdown on the deck of the USS *Bunker Hill* (CVE-17), 26 July 1943.
/US National Archives

Top right: One of VF-17's F4U-1s being catapulted off the deck of the USS *Bunker Hill* (CVE-17) 30 June 1943.
/US National Archives

Bottom right: One of VF-17's F4U-1s picking up a barrier cable and flipping over on its back during the squadron's initial carrier landing qualifications on the USS *Charger* (ACV-30).
/US National Archives

radio channels supersaturated with hyper-excited voices, and all the while the landings continue! With nearly unbelievable courage on both sides, planes bore straight in through ferocious, almost point-blank flak to press home attacks on the ships and enemy planes. One Corsair, probably Ike Kepford, is reported following a torpedo-carrying Kate as it drills in at 20 feet. The Corsair in turn has a Zeke on his tail and somehow splashes the Kate before it can drop its fish, shakes off his pursuer and comes out with only some minor shrapnel holes in his wings.

"My part is plenty exciting, if unproductive. I shag a Zeke from 20,000 to 1,000 feet only to have him gain cloud cover before I can get close enough to shoot, and become the hunted rather than the hunter. My windshield and canopy completely fog over in the hot humid air at low altitude, so I duck into a cloud while it clears, losing contact with my wingman Doug Gutenkunst in the process. As soon as I poke my nose out of the cloud, I spot a flight of six Tonys 5,000 feet above me. They see me and peel off for the kill. Frantically, I get back into the soup before the leader gets in firing range. Scared is a mild word. I next emerge where Roger Hedrick, my Executive Officer, expected a Jap to show, and he reflexes with a beautiful full deflection shot — three bullets through the engine accessory section and three through the fuselage behind the cockpit. Noisy as well as terrifying. At this point

the action is over, and I happily join up with him and his wingman and return to Ondonga.

"Our score for the day is 18 kills with one loss, Windy Hill, who is knocked down by a fighter but unhurt, is picked up by one of our submarines, and returned via PT boat with a tall tale to tell a few days later.

"New Year's Day, 1943, at 8am found me and ten ensigns fresh out of flight training — along with eight enlisted men — shivering in an empty drafty hangar at East Field, Norfolk, somewhat the worse for wear from bringing in the New Year. This considerably less than joyous occasion was for me to read my orders and as CO, declare that VF-17 was thereby formed and commissioned.

"The ranks swelled rapidly, until by the middle of the month we were essentially up to our full strength of 42 pilots, 2 ground officers, and 18 enlisted men. Aircraft maintenance and ordnance support was provided by a Carrier Aircraft Service Unit, a large autonomous command that took care of numerous other squadrons as well as us. This was designed to provide flexibility, so that a squadron could move aboard ship where another similar unit had been, and take over their function without the necessity of moving numerous men and the mountains of equipment and tools. The theory was great, but in practice was very difficult with the split of authority and responsibility, and a complete lack of the espirit de corps which had made the pre-

war carrier squadrons so effective and efficient with their integral ground crews using far fewer men.

"In early March, I went to Naval Air Station Floyd Bennett Field, New York, to pick up the first of our new F4U Corsairs. After checking it over *very* carefully, I was always skittish with a type that was new to me, I radioed for and got takeoff clearance. The runway was bare, but snow was banked six feet high along either edge. With a Grumman Wildcat, the takeoff technique demanded full right rudder until the plane had fifty knots or so of relative wind. With my brand new Corsair, I gave it full throttle, kicked the right rudder pedal to its stop, and started swinging rapidly to starboard for the snow and disaster. I kicked hard left and overcorrected badly and I was now headed for the snow pile on *that* side! Getting it all together took a bit of doing and I was breathing heavily and sweating by the time I got safely airborne. Lesson number one. I then flew it to East Field, Norfolk, and when I taxied up to the flight line, I was greeted by an enthusiastic crowd, all of whom were eager to look over the new plane.

"After a day of preflight preparation, including the painting of 17-F-1 on the sides of the fuselage and putting the pirate flag squadron insignia on the sides of the nose cowling, it was a great occasion to start it up and taxi it out for the first flight in the local area. Deliveries of the new planes seemed maddeningly slow but by the end of the month, we had

49

Bottom left: One of the VF-17s F4U-1s taking off from the USS *Charger* (ACV-30) during the squadron's initial carrier landing qualifications, 8 March 1943. /US National Archives

Bottom right: One of VF-17's F4U-1s about to touchdown on the deck of the USS *Bunker Hill* (CVE-17), 11 July 1943. /US National Archives

Below: The leading ace of VF-17 was Lieutenant Ira C. 'Ike' Kepford with 16 kills, shown here flying his raised canopy F4U-1 near Bougainville, in the Solomon Islands, March 1944./US National Archives

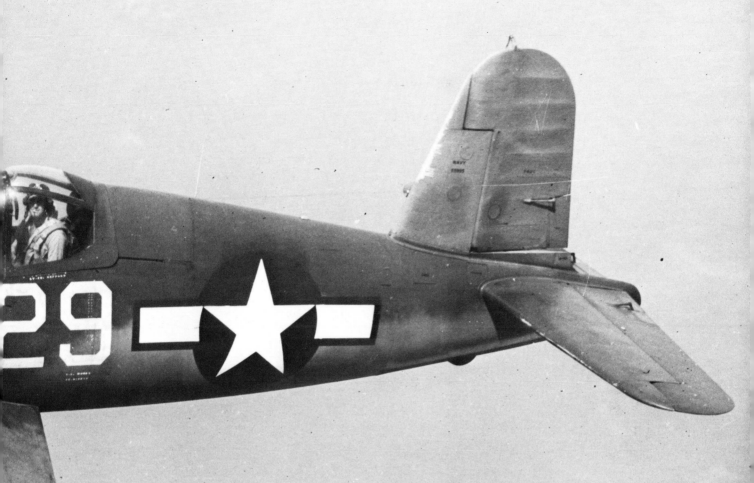

some eighteen in commission and operating, and were busily engaged in checking out our pilots in the planes. This check out procedure occurred at the outset with no real difficulties or accidents which, unfortunately, was not the case as time progressed.

"We experienced numerous mechanical difficulties with the new planes. For example, hydraulic leaks which you wouldn't believe, and voltage regulators that caused storage batteries in the airplanes to overheat and blow up. At this stage, the F4U was an engineer's dream and an operator's nightmare.

"During our period of training at Manteo, North Carolina, which lasted into the summer, we lost six pilots in operational accidents. The F4U was a good machine to fly, but it was unforgiving of pilot error. It had a nasty bounce characteristic on landing, which made the carrier work tough, and virtually no stall warning, so that several people were killed when they got too slow and the plane snapped off into a spin at low altitude.

"I did the experimental work on carrier approaches and landings with the USS *Bunker Hill's* Landing Signal Officer Shailer 'Catwalk' Cummings. After ten or so field practice sessions, we decided that we were ready and set up a test-type operation aboard the jeep carrier USS *Charger*. This was a converted merchantman which operated in the Chesapeake Bay because of the U-Boat threat in the Atlantic. The flight deck of the *Charger* was some fifty feet wide, and with the long nose of the Corsair pointed up during the approach, all I could see on the final straight part of the approach was 'Catwalk' with his paddles out on his platform over the water. On my first try, when he swept his right paddle across his throat in the 'cut' signal, I chopped the throttle and abruptly pushed the stick forward. This was a mistake. I got the view of the flight deck ahead that I so desperately wanted, but also set up an ungodly sink rate. I hit on three points with a teeth rattling jolt and bounced up a good twenty feet. Fortunately, or perhaps unfortunately, my arresting hook had picked up an arresting cable and this snapped the plane back down on the deck even harder than that first ferocious impact, blowing out both main tyres.

After replacing the flats and checking carefully for structural damage, none of which was found, we resumed operations. With six more landings my technique improved so that the last few weren't spectacular controlled crashes like the

first, and it was decided that the F4U was okay for carrier work. But it wasn't going to be easy.

"As soon as the pilots had sufficient flight time in the Corsair they started intensive Field Carrier Landing Practice until each man and 'Catwalk' agreed that they were ready to do the real thing aboard the *Charger*. These landings were major psychological and skill hurdles, but went without serious aircraft damage or pilot injuries. Since it was significantly more difficult to land on a jeep carrier than on the much larger *Essex* class carrier (which would be our future home), when people were qualified to land and takeoff from the very small jeep carrier, they had relatively little trouble operating off the *Bunker Hill*.

"In late June, we went aboard the USS *Bunker Hill*, which was newly completed, and set sail for Trinidad where our ship and its air group would conduct shakedown in the Gulf of Paria. Captain John Ballentine of the *Bunker Hill* was an expert pilot himself, a superb ship handler, and all in all a very fine person to work for. He observed all the air activities very closely. With two new and untried types of aircraft aboard, our Corsairs and the dive-bomber squadron's Curtis Helldivers, there were numerous material difficulties and some question as to what types would be used aboard ship when we sailed for the Pacific in September. During our shakedown, we had numerous accidents with our F4Us, primarily because of the bad bounce characteristic, but also because the arresting hook design was defective. These hooks dug

into the soft fir planking of the flight deck. When they encountered a metal cross deck drain, the point of the hook would snap off. And thus the airplane countinued unchecked up the flight deck until it hit the barrier cables, where it would flip over on its back, doing major damage to the aircraft and scaring the be-Jesus out of everybody concerned. Fortunately, we didn't lose or injure any people in this type of accident, but obviously it was something that we couldn't put up with for fleet operations.

"Chance Vought Aircraft being well aware of the operational difficulties we had encountered with the plane — the hydraulic leaks, the poor forward visibility, the bounce problem, the stall characteristics and this defective hook design — was hard at work making modifications which could not be effected until after we got back from the shakedown cruise. There was serious question as to whether or not the planes were in fact suitable, or could be made so. I was able to convince Captain Ballentine that our troubles could and would be corrected, and that we would have a highly satisfactory operational aircraft to take out to the Pacific. It wasn't until the end of the shakedown cruise, which took about a month, that Captain Ballentine finally sent a dispatch to Commander Air Force, Atlantic Fleet, affirming the decision to stay with the F4Us and not replace them with the lower performance Hellcat. I felt that his decision was made in large measure on the basis of confidence in me and the other pilots of VF-17 and our enthusiasm for the plane.

Top left: Lieutenant Commander John T. 'Tommy' Blackburn, the CO of VF-17, in front of the squadron's operations hut on Bougainville, 19 February, 1944.
/US Navy via Tom Blackburn

Centre left: Immediately after returning to Bougainville, an obviously elated Ensign Andy Jagger related the action of the 19 February 1944, raid on Rabaul to Harry A. 'Eddie' March.
/US Navy via Tom Blackburn

Bottom left: 'Ike' Kepford in the cockpit of his F4U-1 on Bougainville just before takeoff on his 'Adventure Day', 19 February 1944.
/US Navy via Tom Blackburn

Above: Daniel G. 'Danny' Cunningham describing his part in the action over Rabaul on 19 February, to VF-17's Air Combat Intelligence Officer, Basil 'Duke' Henning. On that day, Cunningham shot down four Zekes, raising his total number of kills to seven, making him an Ace.
/US Navy via Tom Blackburn

It was a great morale booster when his decision was finally made and we knew that we could stay with our beloved Corsairs and not have to settle for something less.

"Upon returning to Norfolk, we turned in our first batch of planes, or what was left of them, and received the modified version which had a different cockpit design with vastly improved visibility, with most of the hydraulic problems rectified, with the nasty bounce characteristics eliminated, and with a modification to the wing. This last modification was really quite minor, but in some measure eliminated the dangerous stall characteristics so that one had some warning of impending stall. The stall-spin accidents with the Corsair dropped off very sharply as a result of the change.

"We left Norfolk in early September bound for the Panama Canal. I was so convinced that our plane was improved that I had a ten dollar bet with Captain Ballentine that we wouldn't damage airplanes during the operation en route to the West Coast, nor would we blow more than ten main tyres in the course of the first two hundred landings. On my first landing with the new plane after this bet was made, much to my chagrin and Ballentine's amusement, I managed to blow a tyre. This was one of five that we blew in landing operations during our trip to the West Coast. So I was able to collect the ten bucks from the skipper, which he was happy to pay.

"For efficient utilisation of shipping, numerous spare aircraft and ground equipment were loaded aboard *Bunker Hill* at North Island, San Diego, prior to sailing for Pearl Harbour in September, so that the flight deck was absolutely full and there could be no operations. During the trip to Pearl, we got a dispatch from the Navy Department directing that VF-17 be detached from the *Bunker Hill*, and ordered to report to Commander Aircraft Solomon Islands for duty as a land-based squadron. The reason for this shift was that we were the only US Navy Corsair squadron in the forward area at this time, and it was felt in Washington that the problem of logistic support would be overly complicated by having a different type of aircaft when all the other carriers had Hellcats. This was a great blow because we felt very much a part of the ship and of the air group, and had worked hard to get this position. We were loved and respected by all hands on the ship, including Captain Ballentine. However, there was no arguing about the decision,

so when we got to Pearl, our planes were hoisted off and we bade goodbye.

"We spent a week shorebased at Pearl. We were then hoisted aboard a jeep carrier, the USS *Prince William*, for transportation to Espiritu Santo in the New Hebrides. We were catapulted off the *Prince William* near Espiritu and flew into a field there, Bomber Strip No 1. This was our first acquaintance with landing on Marston matting, which is pierced steel planking laid on the ground to form a landing strip when coral wasn't readily available. It's quite a sensation when you first land on it because it sounds like a series of automobile crashes are occurring as the wheels go over the matting. When the plane touches down at high speed, braking action is minimal and this can be exciting, especially if the landing strip is wet.

"After a few days at Espiritu, we flew some 400 miles up to Guadalcanal, refuelled, were briefed by the Staff of Commander Naval Air Force South Pacific, Vice Admiral Aubrey 'Jakey' Fitch, and then proceeded to our new home at Ondonga, New Georgia, which is adjacent to Munda in the Northern Solomons. This was a coral strip built where a wide lane had been hacked out of a coconut plantation, as were most of the strips in that area. The coral strips were built by first levelling the area, then live coral was dredged from a nearby reef. It was rolled, wet down, and re-rolled until it formed a hard, rough-textured smooth surface. In addition to strength and durability, coral strips possessed high light reflectivity which helped night landings and takeoffs, and provided excellent traction when wet. Finally, the price was right. On the field, in addition to ourselves, were based two New Zealand squadrons flying P-40 Kittyhawks and a

US Army Air Corps squadron flying P-39 Airacobras. Needless to say there was considerable jealousy from the pilots of these squadrons because of our new high performance aircraft, which were far superior to the junk heaps they were taking into combat.

"We used carrier type traffic patterns at Ondonga as we had at Manteo, and of course, when we were aboard ship. For takeoff, we'd veer right for 100 yards to clear the slip stream from the runway for the benefit of the next plane; and the flight leader would proceed straight ahead on takeoff course for four minutes before executing an easy 180 degree turn at 1,000 feet. Thirty second takeoff intervals permitted the whole eight-plane unit to be comfortably joined up in formation passing the field heading downwind, before making a precision departure. This sort of flight discipline was part of the reason that we lost no one due to collisions with mountains at night or in foul weather. For landings, with eight planes for example, the flight came over the strip into the wind with the first four planes in right echelon with wheels down. At the upwind end of the strip, the flight leader would peel off and be followed by the remaining three at thirty second intervals. As the first plane touched down, the second four had circled back to the break-up point and followed suit. As in carrier operations, the approach, except for the last 200 yards, was made in a turn. This was to avoid the turbulence from the plane ahead and to provide good visibility. Propeller fighters were never noted for good forward visibility during landing approaches, and the Corsair was among the worst in this department. Our Air Corps counterparts thought we were nuts to use these techniques which they considered

Top left: 'Tommy' Blackburn's F4U-1 'Big Hog', on Bougainville, 19 February 1944. His airplane is believed to have been the only VF-17 Corsair to have had its number painted under the cowl. */US Navy via Tom Blackburn*

Bottom left: Lieutenant Commander John T. 'Tommy' Blackburn (L) and J. J. 'Jack' Hospers, Chief Field Service Representative for Chance Vought Aircraft, standing beside Blackburn's F4U-1 'Big Hog', at Ondonga, on New Georgia Island, November 1943. The bullet holes that resulted from Roger Hedricks accidental attempt to shoot Blackburn down on 11 November have just been recently patched (between Blackburn and Hospers). */US Navy via Tom Blackburn*

Below: 'Ike' Kepford's F4U-1 parked on Bougainville, 19 February 1944. */US National Archives*

hazardous, but came to see that they were safe and got us up or down, as appropriate, quickly and efficiently.

"At Ondonga, our planes were maintained by Marine ground crews from VMF-215, whose planes and pilots were then in a rear area. These men took us in as if we were their own and kept our planes in beautiful condition. Our operations out of this field were intense. For example, I flew 150 combat hours in a little over a month, and my flight time was not significantly more than any other pilot, except for the ones who were in a 'spare' status and who didn't fly as much.

"On 1 November 1943, the landings were made at Empress Augusta Bay on Bougainville, and we were sent up to provide part of the air cover for these landings. Other fighter cover was provided by squadrons from Munda, the Russell Islands, and Vella Lavella. We were unable to establish voice radio contact with fighter directors aboard the ships, but we could hear some of their radio transmissions to each other. The effectiveness of fighter cover operations of this kind is increased immeasurably by the use of land or ship based radars, by plotting facilities and by capable fighter director personnel. They provide their own planes with information on incoming enemy planes and as their name implies, position the former to facilitate intercept and attack. A major factor in the Battle of Britain was the highly effective control of the British fighters by their fighter directors.

"I had a flight of Corsairs at about

Above, right: VF-17 Corsairs taxi out of their parking area on Bougainville for a raid on the Japanese stronghold at Rabaul, on New Britain Island, 19 February 1944. The ground crewmen sitting on the wing tips helped guide the pilots as they taxied out to the runway. */US Navy via Tom Blackburn;/US National Archives*

Far right: 'Ike' Kepford leading a division of VF-17 Corsairs near Bougainville, in the Solomon Islands, March 1944. */US National Archives*

Above: VF-17 squadron pilots and USMC ground crew alike were all on hand to greet 'Ike' Kepford after his long overdue arrival at Bougainville on his 'Adventure Day', 19 February 1944.
/US Navy via Tom Blackburn

15,000 feet when the ship's radios started chattering about an incoming raid. We were scanning the skies trying to find it, and I spotted off to the east, into the sun, what appeared to be enemy aircraft. We closed as rapidly as possible and it turned out to be Jap divebombers in tight formation covered by a dozen Zeros, also in tight formation, just above them. It looked like a real trap in that the Japs frequently would have formations like this as bait, with 30 or 40 additional fighters up sun from the formation at a higher altitude, waiting to clobber anybody who attacked the tight formation. I alerted the other seven people in my flight by firing my guns and pointing because my radio transmitter wouldn't work at this critical time. We came in at a very high speed on these two formations, directing the attack at the fighters. The Jap squadron leader saw us before we got into firing position, alerted his people, and then peeled out in a climbing turn into us as we closed. We got shots at high speed head-on at these fighters as we came in, but as far as I can tell, we didn't destroy anybody at this point. What resulted subsequently to this was a melee as we pulled up from our dive on this formation. Planes got scattered, and I swung back still looking for my wingman who had gotten separated from me. I made a stern run on a Zero and had the satisfaction of seeing him blow up very close in front of me — close enough so that hydraulic fluid and oil from his aircraft were all over my windshield. (It has been accurately said that your reaction to your first aerial combat kill is like that you experience with your first

piece of ass.) At this point, my wingman and I got back together. The Japs had fled for Rabaul. We found no other Corsairs that we could join up with, so we circled over the landing area conserving fuel and looking for friends or trouble before we were ready to return to Ondonga, 200 miles to the south. We saw a lone P-40 at low altitude being overtaken by a Zero. We dove down, and I was able to get to the Zero and blow him up before he could get a shot at the P-40. We then returned to Ondonga and landed.

"During the relatively quiet days toward the end of November at Ondonga, we had dreamed up the idea of carrying a bomb on our Corsairs. We attached cables to the catapult hook fittings on the bottom of the aircraft and so supported a 500 pounder. This was a hazardous rig at best. We had ideas that we could use our talents for low level flying by doing some skip bombing when there wasn't enemy air opposition to keep us busy. We tried this out and it worked, but when we got back to the rear area, the engineering types were horrified by the thing and insisted that a better design be made which they proceeded to whip up during our period in the rear area. We were able to carry a 500lb bomb for low level attacks after air opposition at Rabaul had diminished.

"In summation of our activities while at Ondonga, New Georgia; we shot down 48 enemy aircraft; lost four pilots and ten aircraft. One pilot was so badly hurt that he had to be sent home. The only other injuries received by pilots were not significantly serious enough to keep them off flying status for a week. We averaged

Above: USMC ground crewmen relaxing in the shade of a VF-17 Corsair's wing on Bougainville, 19 February 1944. The stall strip that was installed to improve the airplane's poor stalling characteristics was mounted on the leading edge of the starboard wing, just outboard of the machine gun ports.
/US Navy via Tom Blackburn

about 100 hours of combat flight time per pilot in a little over five weeks, which is high.

"One of the things we griped about in the forward area was the fact that we had no beer available, and not much hard liquor either. So when we got back from our rest and recreation in Sydney, we took up a collection among the pilots and bought 148 cases of beer which were stored under lock and key in the big Quonset hut which Roger Hedrick and I shared. It was great to have this beer, and we looked forward to having it on Bougainville, but we couldn't figure out how to get it up there safely. We were wise in the ways of operations in the South Pacific by this time and knew if we put it aboard ship, it would be stolen. We also knew that we couldn't get by with boxing it and labelling it 'Electronic Parts' and then getting it air shipped up to Bougainville. Then Hal Jackson had a bright idea and came bursting into Rog's and my quonset one day, hollering, 'I got it Skipper, I got it'. He then outlined his plan which we put into effect. The plan was that we would use four of the six ammunition boxes in each wing of the Corsair to carry the beer. As Hal said, 'Then we would have four guns operable with 200 rounds per gun. This would be plenty for our flight into the forward area. We never had any more than 16 planes together in a flight, and we've taken on as many as 80 Japs at once successfully. This way, with 32 planes in formation there shouldn't be any sweat.' Rog and I agreed. So, when we took off from Espiritu we had the planes loaded accordingly, and each pilot was equipped

with a beer can-opener. For the last leg of our flight to Bougainville, I took the squadron up to 20,000 feet for about the last 45 minutes where the air was good and cold. We landed at Bougainville, taxied into the revetments, and as the ground crewmen climbed on to the aircraft to help the pilot get out of his chute and plane, he was greeted with a beer can-opener and asked to open one of the ammunition compartments in the wing and have a cold beer with the pilot. I know of no refusals. We were in like Flynn with the ground crews from here on out for our consideration and throughtfulness. We had beer to last for a while, but hardly indefinitely.

"We went into Bougainville on 26 January 1944, with 36 aircraft, 42 pilots and almost immediately the action became intense. We were flying from Bougainville escorting bombers in raids on the Jap stronghold at Rabaul, where they had five airfields, a beautiful harbour, and a good radar installation that was used to spot us coming in and to control their fighters, as well as an enormous concentration of anti-aircraft weapons. We would fly raids against Rabaul daily. One day would be dedicated to high altitude horizontal bombing against the airfields by B-24s or B-25s. On the alternate days, strikes were made against the aircraft in revetments on the airfields by our dive-bombers and torpedo planes. There was probably no element of surprise. Their own people on Bougainville reported when we took off, how many took off, and when to expect us. Consequently, as we approached on these strikes, we were greeted by intense enemy aircraft opposition. We were tied to the bombers and had to protect them and ourselves as best we could, and tangle with the Japs in the process. It was a very rough go. On these raids, we normally had 16 of our own F4Us as part of a 60- to 72-plane fighter cover for the bombers. The melees were almost indescribable and were twenty to thirty minutes in length. It seemed like a lot shorter time, but they were exhausting minutes because of the intense activity.

"We went in with 42 pilots and we were supposed to stay 42 days. Our squadron's average loss rate the first ten days was one per day, and it didn't take a mathematician to figure out what the probability was for each guy who went in, initially. This did nothing to help morale, even though we were knocking the Japanese planes down in great numbers.

"As we pulled out from these raids, the Jap fighters would break away from us when we were about ten miles south of the coastline, and we could see them returning to their own fields to land. This gave us the bright idea for a so-called 'Statue of Liberty' play. This was named after the American football oldie in which a back would stand with his arm cocked as if to pass; then the left end would swing behind him, pick off the ball and run around right end, sometimes unopposed.

"Ours worked like this. After the bombers were safely on their way home, we took eight planes down to low level, and swung off to the east. We then proceeded north with the island of New Ireland between us and Rabaul, to a position northeast of Rabaul. Then we flew up over New Ireland, across St. George's Channel, and were able to come in on the airfields from what they thought was the 'safe' northerly direction. They didn't expect us and we made a low level high-speed attack on the Jap aircraft which were landing to refuel and re-arm after returning from the flight they had made to counter the bomber attack. We scattered it out so we were able to effect surprise each time we tried it. And we caught quite a few sitting ducks as the planes were coming in ready to land with their wheels and flaps down. It was a single pass at maximum speed, then we headed home before they could react.

"Ike Kepford had a harrowing adventure on the last day of aircraft operations over Rabaul. He came into the danger area late trying to catch up with the formation (which was against our policy). He then developed oxygen trouble and elected to try and follow at low altitude. He caught site of a Rufe floatplane fighter, and shot it down. Almost immediately, he saw 20 Japanese fighters coming out of a cloud at 16,000 feet. Four of them dropped down and made a stern run on him. Kepford extended his flaps, and the first Zeke overran him. As the Zeke pulled up, Ike got in a burst and sent the plane down in flames. The three remaining Jap fighters pursued him as he headed north trying to outrun them, and at the same time, catch up with the rest of the flight. Meanwhile, he was trying to inform me as to his position so that possibly I could send some planes to help him, which I was unable to do. The last that we heard from Ike at this point was that he was heading north at full throttle with three Japs holding their own behind him. We did not expect to see him again. It turned out that his fuel was so low that he began to question whether of not he would get home. At that moment, he decided he had to break for it. The three fighters were in line abreast astern of him. He turned suddenly, as tightly as he could, back toward his pursuers. In his eagerness to get at Ike, the one on the side toward which he turned dug a wing tip into the water, and cartwheeled and crashed. Ike was able to get around the other two and came back to the strip at Bougainville after we had long since given up hope for him. Ike was no pantywaist, but he was shaken up almost beyond belief by his protracted ordeal. And it took several days with medication and a lot of talk from Duke Henning, the flight surgeon Lyle Hermann, and from me

Below: USMC Corsairs parked on Bougainville, 19 February 1944. /*US National Archives*

before he calmed down and was able to resume flight activities.

"Our last air to air combat occurred in the middle of February. We were escorting dive-bombers and torpedo planes in the usual strikes against Rabaul and were met by fierce opposition. We had a high score for one day, 13 kills. Danny Cunningham achieved one of these without firing a shot. A Zero at low altitude was flying at right angles to Danny, and apparently didn't spot him soon enough. When Dan was just about to open fire, the Jap saw him and took evasive action by attempting a diving turn in his direction. Much to his misfortune, however, he started his diving turn from forty feet altitude, and sliced into the water. Properly enough, Dan claimed him as a kill, saying that his ugly Irish visage, complete with heavy black beard, was enough to scare anybody to death.

"The following day we went up with the high altitude bomber raid as was the usual rotation, to find absolutely no air opposition, and we were also unable to spot any aircraft on the ground. The Japs had pulled all their planes out of Rabaul and had taken them back to Kavieng, which was 200 miles to the north, and to Truk, in the Carolina Islands.

"After a couple of days of this inactivity, we were authorised by AirSols to hang bombs on our planes. These were delay-fused for attack against shipping, and could also be used for skip bombing at low altitudes against land surface targets. The fusing was such that it provided sufficient delay after bomb

impact before explosion for the attacking plane to fly clear. We stooged around the Rabaul area staying away from the AA batteries and bombed one factory. The balance of our stay on Bougainville was uneventful.

"In retrospect, what I believe we had done with fighting 17 was significant in that we did set a record in the South Pacific for the number of kills for one squadron. Admittedly, we had the best aircraft in the area and came in under optimum conditions. What's more, we proudly boasted that no ship under our cover was ever hit by an enemy bomb or torpedo and that none of the aircraft on which we flew cover was destroyed by enemy planes. This fundamentally was our mission: the protection of the ships and of the aircraft and home areas. We batted a thousand in this department, as well as in setting the record for kills. It was subsequently broken by other squadrons, and broken very significantly.

"When we got our Corsairs, we were one of the two Navy squadrons initially assigned that plane. We were the squadron that continued with it and proved it out as successful and usable in carrier operations, for which, later in the war, it was employed extensively. The subsequent model F4U-4 became the Navy's basic fighter until it was replaced by the jets starting at the end of the 1940s. We developed cruise control techniques for the Corsair which Charles Lindbergh (then employed by United Aircraft) later refined. The cruise control techniques extended the range of the plane well beyond what was thought possible when we started out. In large measure this was due to Butch Davenport's experiments in operating at low altitudes with very low engine speeds and determining optimum speeds to produce both maximum endurance and greatest range. Cruise control was a significant and valuable contribution which was used extensively and was later adapted to other types of prop-driven aircraft. Our brainstorm about putting bombs on the Corsair worked too, and was effective. The airplane was further modified for both bombs and drop tanks. By using the landing gear as a divebrake, the Corsair proved to be quite an effective divebomber, in additon to its great utility as a fighter.

"Our bent-wing bird not only became a mainstay of carrier squadrons during the latter part of the war, but endured beyond to play a valuable role in the Korean conflict before being put out to pasture like its hot pilots."

Below: 'Ike' Kepford taxiing out of the parking area on Bougainville before his 'Adventure Day' mission on 19 February 1944./ *US National Archives*

Tests and Modifications Continue

Detailed improvements on the Corsair continued. The first F4U-1 equipped with the new raised canopy installation (F4U-1 No. 950) was accepted by the Navy on 9 August 1943. The first F4U-1 with provisions for mounting a centre-line 170-gallon drop tank was delivered to the Navy on 5 October 1943. This feature was incorporated on F4U-1 No. 1302 and on, and FG-1 No. 581 and on. On 25 November, the Navy received the first Corsair (F4U-1 No. 1551) equipped with an R-2800-8W engine, which incorporated a water injection system. The water injection could be used for very short durations to boost the maximum power of the engine to 2,230hp at sea level. This additional horsepower increased the Corsair's maximum speed to 415mph at 20,000 feet, and its sea level rate of climb to 3,120 feet per minute. All subsequent F4U-1s, as well as FG-1 No. 1001 and on,

and F3A-1 No. 650 and on, were equipped with the R-2800-8W engine. Both of these modifications were later incorporated in the next production versions of the Corsair, the F4U-1C the F4U-1D and FG-1D.

A total of 2,294 Corsairs were built in 1943. Vought produced 1,780; Brewster, 136; and Goodyear, 378.

During 1944, the Marine Corps' top fighter was to come into its own with the US Navy. But a long, uphill battle for acceptance lay ahead. Although Corsairs were being operated successfully from carriers by the British, and were also highly praised as a land-based weapon, the US Navy was not ready to use the Corsair as a carrier fighter. In March 1944, the Chief of Naval Air Operational Training, Jacksonville, Florida, drafted a letter in which he condemned the Corsair's deck-landing characteristics.

Right, far right: A side view comparison of a Corsair I and II (F4U-1s), the Corsair I with the later type 'Birdcage' canopy which incorporated a rear view mirror; the Corsair II with the new raised canopy. The pilot's seat height was also increased seven inches in the raised canopy version to improve visibility further./*US National Archives*

His prime reason for the condemnation was that the F4U-1, especially in the hands of inexperienced pilots, tended to bounce dangerously on landing. Had the letter been dispatched, the Corsair probably would have been ruled out for all time as a carrier-based fighter. However, because of the efforts of Chance Vought's Jack Hospers, Captain John Pearson, Fighter Design Officer in the Bureau of Aeronautics, and Captain H. S. Duckworth, Chief of Staff, Fleet Air Jacksonville, the letter was held back.

'Program Dog' was instituted immediately and the letter was never sent. This programme, one of four that Vought engineers proposed, took just ten days to implement. It went right to the heart of the problem — improving the rebound characteristics of the main landing gear oleos. With this modification, the built-in bounce of the Corsair was eliminated once and for all. (A similar modification was incorporated on VF-17's Corsairs in September 1943.) The results of test flights with the improved landing gear were so successful that the airplane was immediately endorsed by the Commander Fleet Air, Jacksonville.

All stigma attached to the Corsair's landing characteristics was erased aboard the carrier USS *Gambier Bay* in April 1944. Navy Fighter Squadron VF-301, equipped with F4U-1s which had the

Above: A flight of raised canopy Goodyear Aircraft FG-1 Corsairs. The FG-1 was intended for exclusive use by land-based USMC squadrons, and did not have carrier arresting gear or provisions for wing folding. /*Goodyear Aircraft*

Above: A factory fresh F4U-1 with a centre-line Duramold 178-gallon drop tank sports a pristine three-tone counter-shading, counter-shadowing paint job that was specified for the January 1943-June 1944 time period. The upper wing and upper horizontal tail surfaces were semi-gloss sea blue, and the upper fuselage surface was non-specular sea blue. The fuselage sides, lower wing surface outboard of the wing fold line, vertical stabiliser and rudder were non-specular intermediate blue. The lower fuselage, lower wing surface inboard of the wing fold line and lower horizontal tail surfaces were non-specular insignia white.
/Vought Aircraft via Art Schoeni

Right: An early version of a VMF-222 'Flying Deuces' Corsair's home-made centre-line bomb rack installation. The rack was constructed from iron water pipe by squadron mechanics.
/Jim Sullivan

modified oleo struts, completed 113 landings with excellent results. As a result of the *Gambier Bay* landing trials an order went out to modify the oleo struts on all Corsairs. The Corsairs had finally won complete acceptance by the Navy for carrier duty.

The Corsair performed in the role of divebomber for the first time in March 1944, when eight VMF-111 Corsairs, each equipped with homemade bomb racks and carrying a 1,000lb bomb, struck anti-aircraft positons on Mille Island in the Marshalls. VF-17 had begun similar experiments four months earlier with Rabaul as their target. During the seven weeks following this baptism as a fighter-bomber, Corsairs dropped more than 200,000lbs of bombs on Japanese installations in the Marshalls. The homemade bomb racks were later replaced with a more substantial rack designed by Brewster.

Air Operations Memorandum No. 30
8 May 1944
The F4U as a Dive Bomber
Latest among the fighters to carry bombs is the F4U. Recent action reports from Marine F4U squadrons which have been unloading 500 and 1,000lb bombs on remaining Japanese bases in the

Marshalls indicate pilots in many cases are initiating dive-bombing runs from 10,000 feet and pulling out at 5,000 feet after bomb release. Dives range in angles up to 75 degrees and apparently are made without the braking effect of a lowered landing gear.

Training experience with the F4Us indicate that pullouts at 5,000 feet do not produce the accuracy obtainable in a well executed dive-bombing run. By lowering the landing gear, Corsairs can execute a 70-degree dive, drop bombs at 2,500 feet and, with a five-g pullout, can attain level flight at 1,800 feet.

Air Operations Memorandum No. 33
4 June 1944
More on Low-Level Bombing by Corsairs
Since the first reports of low-level bombing by F4Us of VMF-224, the pilots of the squadron have been working steadily with the new technique against targets on remaining Japanese Marshalls bases. Some of the conclusions reached on the basis of these missions are as follows:
Tactics
Results of attacks show that in hitting sturdy targets such as concrete block houses, it is essential that bombs hit the target directly. Skip or bounce must be eliminated. On one mission, two GP

Above: Fourth Marine Air Wing Corsairs on a strike against Japanese targets in the Marshall Islands, 1944.
/USMC via Rowland Gill

Right, far right: USMC Corsairs loaded with 500lb bombs taxi from their parking area on Majuro Atoll, in the Marshall Islands, August 1944.
/US National Archives

Below: White-nosed VMF-114 'Death Dealers' Corsairs loaded with 500lb bombs taxi out on Peleliu, in the Palau Group, for a strike against Babelthuap, another island in the Palau Group, 17 October 1944.
/USMC via Rowland Gill

bombs hit the side of the target directly and penetrated the thick walls, while one bomb which skipped into the block house simply fell off the wall and exploded at the base doing some, but not lethal, damage.

In a typical successful approach, the fighter-bombers made their dives from 8,000 feet at an approximate dive angle of 45 degrees and started gradually pulling out at 800 to 1,000 feet until they were in an attitude of approximately 10 degrees. This angle was held on into the target, with the pipper at the base of the target. As the target started dropping under the nose, planes pulled up slightly and released. Speed and changes of altitude were principal evasive tactics in the retirement. Pilots emphasise the necessity for starting the gradual pullout from the initial steep dive soon enough so that in the last stages of approach, the plane is in a 10-degree nose down attitude. This gives ample time for lining up the pipper and also reduces the trajectory of the bomb. It also enables the pilot to build up and maintain greater speed.

Support by Strafers

Low-level bombing is done in four-plane sections. On the first missions, each plane

picked up two strafers, one on either wing, and these followed the bomber down throughout the dive and the run over the target, firing to discourage AA opposition.

Several factors, however, led the pilots of the fighter-bombers to shy away from this formation support strafing on subsequent missions. First, the AA encountered was light and very meagre, ceasing entirely when the first bomb was dropped. Second, the high speed of the bombing planes over the target and in the get-away eliminates much of the risk from AA. A third point is the intense concentration required to accomplish precision bombing, a precision which easily can be spoiled by a single mistake on the part of the accompanying strafers. One of the bombing Corsairs returned with a .50-calibre slug in his wing, the slug apparently having ricocheted off the ground after being fired by the strafer flying with him. For obvious reasons, the bombing pilots prefer not to have any such distractions. Likewise, they prefer to do no strafing themselves during the bombing run.

Type of Bombs

On the basis of results to date, the 1,000lb GP is preferred over the SAP for heavily reinforced targets. Prior to trials, it was thought the GP might break up without penetrating when it hit the target, but it was found that it did penetrate when lined up for a direct hit on the side of the target. Although none of the SAP's used thus far have hit, they do not carry the same explosive weight as the GP, and thus, would be likely to have less effect.

The five-second delay fuzing appears to have a good destructive effect and, at the same time, gives the plane sufficient time to clear the target and avoid being damaged by the explosion. The necessity for leaving the area in a hurry is obvious. One pilot made the mistake of lowering a wing for a look at the results after he had released. His bomb blew up a magazine and the shock of the blast has reformed him as a great believer in the principle of retiring fast and far.

Training

Pilots of VMF-224 are enthusiastic about low-level bombing as is Marine Air Group 31 under which they operate. More opportunity for practice is desired. The more experienced hands all agree that pilots must find out for themselves just what to use for point of aim in order to get hits. Training thus far has been confined to actual missions and what the veterans

Top left: A USMC Corsair pilot gets a 'thumbs up' signal before leaving the parking area on Majuro Atoll, August 1944. */US National Archives*

Bottom left: A flight test F4U-1D fighter-bomber with a load of 1,000lb bombs mounted on the Corsair's wing centre section pylons. */Vought Aircraft via Art Schoeni*

Above: A cannon-armed VMF-311 'Hells Belles' F4U-1C Corsair undergoing repairs at Yonton Airfield on Okinawa, 17 July 1945. */USMC via Rowland Gill*

can tell the others. It is believed that exercises with practice bombs, if they were available, would do much to develop accuracy.

The F4U-1D version of the Corsair started rolling off the assembly lines at Vought in April 1944. The Goodyear version of this airplane, the FG-1D, went into production in September of that same year. (The F3A-1D did not get into production before Brewster went out of business in July 1944.) The first F4U-1D (F4U-1 No. 2815) was delivered to the Fleet Air Arm of the Royal Navy as a Corsair 11, along with the next nine F4U-1Ds produced. Likewise, the first FG-1D (FG-1 No. 2001) was also delivered to the Fleet Air Arm, along with the next batch of 306 produced by Goodyear as Corsair IVs.

The -1D version of the Corsair was equipped for operation as a long range fighter-bomber, with provisions for carrying either two 1,000lb bombs, or two 154-gallon drop tanks on twin pylons that were located beneath the wing centre section. The two outer wing panel fuel tanks were eliminated in the -1D as were

the outer wing panel Mark 41-2 bomb racks. Later, provisions were included in the -1Ds to enable them to carry a load of eight 5-inch rockets by installing four rocket launchers under each outer wing panel. (F4U-1 No. 4100 and on, FG-1 No 2602 and on).

On 16 May 1944, after a series of comprehensive comparisons had been made between the F6F-3 Hellcat and the F4U-1D, a Navy evaluation board stated: 'It is the opinion of the board that generally the F4U is a better fighter, a better bomber and equally suitable carrier airplane as compared with the F6F . . . It is strongly recommended that carrier fighter and/or bomber complements be shifted to the F4U type.' As squadrons returned to the rear areas, they would gradually exchange their F6Fs for newly-arrived Corsairs.

**Air Operations Memorandum No. 33
4 June 1944**
Combat Tests of FW-190 vs F6F-3 and F4U-1
Combat evaluation tests of an FW-190 against an F6F-3 and F4U-1 afford interesting comparisons of Navy and Marine planes with the outstanding enemy fighter in the European theatre. The tests were made at NAS Patuxent

River, Maryland, with new production models of the F6F and F4U airplanes, loaded to gross weights of 12,406 and 11,988 pounds, respectively, and a captured FW-190, previous flight time unknown, loaded to gross weight of 8,690 pounds. Prior to the comparative tests, the FW-190 was stripped and painted with standard smooth camouflage finish. Pilots were familiarised with the airplane. Airspeed indicators in all three planes were calibrated and loads were checked.

Rate of Climb

The FW-190 showed superiority in climb over the F6F at all speeds and altitudes except at 140 knots below 15,000 feet where they were about equal. At 140 knots, the F4U was slightly superior to the FW-190 up to 20,000 feet. At 160 knots, the FW-190 was superior at all altitudes, especially at 15,000 feet. The FW-190 showed marked superiority at 180 and 200 knots up to 10,000 feet, above which altitude its advantage decreased. The best climbing speed for the German plane was 160 knots.

Horizontal Speed

Speed tests were made for periods of two minutes at full available power. Full speed may not have been developed during such short runs, but the following data should serve for the purpose of comparison (all speeds are true airspeed):

Altitude	FW-190	F4U-1	F6F-3
200 feet	290 knots	315 knots	290 knots
5,000	310	314	305
10,000	310	320	302
15,000	335	335	320
20,000	348	343	331
25,000	356	350	339

The 3,608th Vought Corsair was produced in July 1944, and was the first F4U-1C, which was armed with four 20-millimetre M-2 automatic cannons in place of the standard six 50-calibre machine guns. Four ammunition boxes were carried in each wing panel that supplied 220 rounds of ammunition to each cannon. The muzzles of the long-barrelled Hispano cannons protruded well forward of the wing leading edges, and the airplane was particularly well suited for ground strafing missions. F4U-1C production was alternated on the assembly lines with F4U-1Ds in batches varying from 3 to 43. A total of 200 F4U-1Cs were produced, along with 2,814 F4U-1s (949 with the 'birdcage' type canopy), and 1,685 F4U-1Ds. The last F4U-1D was delivered to the Navy on 2 February 1945.

Corsairs with the Royal Navy

Lieutenant Commander (A) Norman S. Hanson, RNVR

Corsairs with the insignia of the Royal Navy first appeared at US Naval Air Station, Quonset Point, Rhode Island on 1 June 1943 when the Fleet Air Arm's No 1830 Squadron (Lieut Commander D. B. M. Fiddes, DSO, RN) arrived to take possession. With them was 1831 Squadron (Lieut Commander Peter Allingham, DSC, RNR). Close on their heels, a month later, arrived Squadrons 1833 (Lieut Commander H. A. Monk, DSM, RN) and 1834 (Lieut Commander (A) A. M. Tritton, DSC, RNVR).

By the end of the year, four more squadrons had been formed. The last of the 19 Fleet Air Arm squadrons to be equipped with Corsairs was formed at US Naval Air Station, Brunswick, Maine in April 1945.

A total of 1,967 Corsairs were delivered to the Fleet Air Arm under the Lend-Lease agreement. These included 95 Vought 'birdcage' canopy F4U-1s,

designated Corsair 1s; 360 raised canopy F4U-1s and 150 F4U-1Ds, which were designated Corsair IIs; 430 Brewster F3A-1s, designated Corsair IIIs; and 405 Goodyear FG-1s and 527 FG-1Ds, designated Corsair IVs.

Familiarisation and training were completed by the Royal Naval squadrons in the US either at Quonset Point or Brunswick before the aircraft were shipped to Great Britain in escort carriers. The pilots then continued their training in the United Kingdom.

Nos 1830, 1831 and 1833 Squadrons returned to the United Kingdom in October 1943, where a brief spell of further training was undertaken. No 1831 Squadron was disbanded and its pilots were re-allocated to 1830 and 1833 Squadrons. At the same time the opportunity was taken to re-equip with British-type VHF radio sets and to fit to the fuselage sides small air-scoops,

Below: Fleet Air Arm (FAA) Corsair Is (F4U-1s) warming up on the flight line at Naval Air Station Brunswick, Maine, September 1943./*US National Archives.*

designed to disperse pockets of carbon monoxide which, so the 'back-room boys' alleged, were liable to accumulate in the fuselage abaft the cockpit. There was some suggestion that the exhaust manifold stubs, flush with the forward part of the fuselage, were not throwing the gases clear. A further modification carried out was a reduction in the wingspan, when eight inches were clipped off each wing to permit below-deck stowage in British carriers. This change produced a slightly higher stalling speed but improved manoeuvrability at lower altitudes.

Deck-landing on a full-sized deck, essayed by the first two squadrons when they joined HMS *Illustrious* in December 1943, proved to be distinctly hazardous. There were several nasty deck 'prangs', one of which brought about the untimely death of the commanding officer of 1830 Squadron. In an endeavour to take a last-minute wave-off from the batsman (landing signal officer) he clipped the port wingtip on the flight deck and crashed over the side, sinking with his aircraft before help could reach him. His death was a bitter blow to the new squadrons and a serious loss to the Service. To replace him, Michael Tritton left 1834 Squadron (newly arrived from the United States) and joined 1830 as commanding officer.

Illustrious' Captain decided that further deck-landing training was

essential. Whilst the carrier remained in the Clyde, therefore, her pilots, together with the ship's senior batsman, were temporarily transferred for a week's intensive training to the escort carrier *Ravager*. The main troubles were first, the poor cockpit hood and low seating position; second, the 'in-built' bounce of the undercarriage; and third, the fact that the current RN landing 'pattern' was totally unsuited to Corsairs. When a new pattern was established, landings improved immediately and the casualty rate dropped. The ensuing months were to prove that truly safe landings would never be achieved until the cockpit and 'bounce' faults were eradicated — which, of course, they eventually were.

Illustrious and her Corsairs sailed for Ceylon in December 1943 and first engaged the enemy in Sumatra on 19 April 1944. In the meantime, however, on 8 March 1944, HMS *Victorious* had embarked Corsair Squadrons 1834 and 1836, commanded by Lieut Commanders P. N. Charlton, RN and Chris Tomkinson, RNVR (A) respectively. With ships of the Home Fleet, she took part in operation 'Tungsten' off Norway, against the German battleship *Tirpitz*. The Corsairs provided fighter cover for torpedo and dive-bombing attacks by Barracudas from *Victorious* and *Furious*. One of the Corsair pilots who took part in that operation was Sub-Lieutenant (A) Derek Robertson, RNVR, of 1836 Squadron,

Below: Armourers loading an FAA Corsair I's (F4U-1) port battery of three 50-calibre machine guns at Naval Air Station Brunswick, Maine, September 1943.
/US National Archives.

which he had joined in the autumn of 1943 straight from flying training.

The first operation against *Tirpitz*, lying in Alten Fjord, took place on 3 April 1944 when Robertson was one of the fighters giving top cover to the Barracudas. They encountered no German fighters and he recalls only the thick murk of the smokescreen surrounding the battleship far below him. On 26 April he accompanied his CO in a sweep over the shipping anchorages off Bodo. In pulling away from an attack on an armed merchantman — possibly a flak-ship — he saw his fuel gauge 'going berserk' and petrol flooding past the perspex window of the cockpit deck. He had no alternative but to ditch. Somewhere near Skomvoer Light, off the southern end of the Lofoten Islands, he saw a fishing fleet. With the eye of a true survivor, he smartly ditched in the middle of the Norwegian fishermen. In a moderate sea and with plenty of engine power burning up the last of his fuel, he put the Corsair into the sea 'with no worse a jar than picking up an arrester wire'. His judgement was good, for the fishermen rescued him safely from his dinghy. He endured a year in a German POW camp in the Oslo area, found himself towards the end of the war in Russian hands and, finally, returned to the United Kingdom none the worse for his adventures.

In spite of his regrettably brief experience in Corsairs, he had the highest regard for them. It may well be that the fact that he had trained on American aircraft at Pensacola and Miami contributed largely to the ease with which he had so readily assimilated the complexities of handling the big fighter.

While *Tirpitz* was still licking her wounds, she was struck again on 17 July 1944 by Barracudas from *Indefatigable* and *Formidable*. The latter carrier was equipped with Corsair Squadrons 1841 and 1842. Further attacks were delivered between 22 and 29 August but, although further hits were registered, it was not until 12 November 1944 that *Tirpitz* was finally destroyed, overwhelmed by the 12000lb bombs from Lancasters of Nos 9 and 617 RAF Squadrons.

Until such time as *Victorious* could be sailed to the Far East to join *Illustrious*, the USS *Saratoga* left her happy hunting grounds at Espiritu Santo and arrived in China Bay on 2 April 1944. Fifteen days later, her Air Group 12 (Hellcats, Dauntlesses and Avengers) joined *Illustrious'* Barracudas and Corsairs in a dawn attack on the harbour and airfield of Sabang, a port at the northern extremity of Sumatra. The aircraft delivered a highly-co-ordinated attack, opposed only by flak which opened fire after the strike was well under way. There was little shipping in the harbour, but one small freighter was sunk and another damaged, oil storage tanks were destroyed and heavy damage was inflicted on the port facilities. In a suppressive sweep over the airfield, the Corsairs and Hellcats destroyed 24 enemy aircraft on the ground.

Below: FAA Corsair Is (F4U-1s)
from Naval Air Station
Brunswick, Maine, September
1943./*US National Archives.*

Bottom: FAA Corsair Is (F4U-1s)
parked at Naval Air Station
Brunswick, Maine, September
1943./*US National Archives*

After returning to Trincomalee, *Saratoga* was ordered to return to the United States for re-fitting. The decision was made to combine her eastward passage with a strike on the important aviation fuel refinery at Sourabaya in Java on 17 May 1944. Avengers from *Illustrious* and Avengers and Dauntlesses from *Saratoga* were escorted by Corsairs and Hellcats, providing cover for the bombers and strafing forces for the town, harbour and industrial areas. Attacking in two waves, one struck at the refinery while the other went for the dockyard and shipping in the harbour. Surprise was again achieved but the results were slender. One small ship was sunk and some damage was done to the refinery and a large Dutch-owned engineering factory on the southern approach to the town. Fighters from both carriers attacked a large airfield at Malang in the centre of Java, on the return journey to the Fleet; they destroyed a considerable number of aircraft and set fire to most of the airfield buildings.

The Corsairs of 1830 and 1833 Squadrons next saw action during a raid on the Andaman Islands on 2 June 1944. Due to bad weather in the target area, the Barracudas had little success against the few targets available. Ten enemy aircraft were destroyed and considerable damage was achieved on installations on the field at Port Blair by strafing Corsairs and a few small coastal vessels were sunk by the dive-bombers.

In early July, *Victorious* and *Indomitable* joined *Illustrious* in the

Eastern Fleet. Their first combined operation was the bombardment of Sabang, the target of the April strike, on 25 July 1944. Most of *Illustrious'* Barracudas were replaced by an additional Corsair Squadron, No 1837, to provide full defensive cover for the attack. In addition to providing gunfire spotting, the Corsairs struck at shipping in the harbour, at shore installations and at airfields. The air strikes again destroyed the oil storage tanks which had been repaired since the previous strike. There was little shipping in the harbour and only two small ships were sunk, with a larger one obliged to ground.

The next large-scale offensive operation by the carrier squadrons was diversionary support for the American forces who were about to start landings in Leyte Gulf. In an attempt to draw off Japanese naval forces, airplanes from *Indomitable* and *Victorious* struck at the Nicobar Islands for the three days preceding the assault on Leyte, simulating a pre-invasion bombardment. The enemy apparently was fully preoccupied with the impending events in the Philippines and there was no obvious reaction to the diversion. Targets were few and far between, although Japanese fighters were encountered. Six Oscar fighters were shot down by Hellcats and Corsairs at no loss to Fleet Air Arm fighters.

Nearly two months passed before the carrier squadrons undertook another operation. Unfortunately their first, on 20 December, was not very successful

because of bad weather. A strike of Avengers, Corsairs and Hellcats from *Indomitable*, *Victorious* and *Illustrious* — now rejoined after a short boiler refit in South Africa — which had set out for the refinery at Pangkalan Brandan in Sumatra was obliged to divert to their secondary target, the port of Belawan Deli, on the Malacca Straits near Medan. Fighters strafed an airfield at Medan and destroyed a few aircraft on the ground. The port was obscured by low clouds and heavy squalls and the strike achieved only modest results. No aircraft were lost and, as the Fleet withdrew, its Corsairs and Hellcats attacked the airfields in the vicinity of Sabang, destroying several Japanese aircraft on the ground. The operation was notable, if for no other reason, in that this was the first occasion on which the Fleet used Corsairs in the fighter-bomber role, several of them being armed with 500lb bombs.

On 4 January 1945 a restrike was made on Pangkalan Brandan. The combined air groups attacked with Avengers and Fireflies, dropping bombs and firing rockets, whilst Corsairs and Hellcats carried out a sweep over the enemy airfields before the strike, as well as providing escort for the strike aircraft. This attack, executed in good weather, was a complete success. Heavy damage was inflicted on the refinery, considerably reducing its output, while the Corsairs and Hellcats destroyed 12 enemy aircraft in air combat and another 20 in stafing attacks on the airfield.

At the end of 1944 the British Pacific

Top left: An FAA Corsair I (F4U-1) from Naval Air Station Brunswick, Maine, September 1943. One unusual feature of this particular aircraft is the absence of both plexiglass at the rear edge of the canopy, and the plexiglass covered cutouts behind the canopy, which were standard on almost all 'Birdcage' canopy versions of the Corsair. */US National Archives.*

Centre left: An FAA Corsair I (F4U-1) parked on an unknown airfield in either England or Scotland./*IWM*

Bottom left: The main landing gear of an FAA Corsair I (F4U-1) is just starting to rotate and retract aft after takeoff from an unknown airfield in either England or Scotland./*IWM*

Above: Preflight engine runs being performed on a new FAA Corsair II (F4U-1) at the Vought plant. */Vought Aircraft via Art Schoeni.*

Above: FAA Corsairs await takeoff aboard an unknown British carrier./*IWM.*

Top right: A Corsair III (Brewster F3A-1) about to touchdown on the company's runway. Of the 735 F3A-1 Corsairs produced by Brewster, 430 were delivered to the Royal Navy.
/*Brewster Aeronautical via Harold Andrews.*

Centre right: An FAA Corsair II (F4U-1) of No 1830 Squadron gets the 'cut' from the batsman as it crosses the stern of HMS *Illustrious.* A continuous-turn approach was preferred by the pilots because of poor forward visibility, and they did not roll wings level until just before touchdown./*IWM*

Bottom right: An FAA Corsair taking off from an unknown British carrier./*IWM*

Fleet was formed and on 16 January 1945 the main striking force left Trincomalee for Sydney, which was to be the Fleet's base for Pacific operations. En route the carriers undertook strikes on the Sumatran oil refineries around Palembang.

The first of these strikes was made on the Pladjoe refinery on 24 January. In an attempt to prevent enemy fighters from reacting in strength, some of the Avengers and part of the fighter escort attacked the major airfields in the target area. The attack was successful and no enemy aircraft were encountered until the Avengers began their deployment for the attack. The output of the refinery was cut in half for three months and most of the oil storage tanks were burned as a result of the attack. Thirty-four aircraft were destroyed on the airfields, but some of the Japanese fighters did manage to get airborne. The escort fighters destroyed 14 enemy aircraft in combat.

Because of launching difficulties, the bow escort of 12 Fireflies left *Indefatigable* long after the main strike had disappeared towards the mountains of Sumatra and joined only at the tail-end of the action. Lieut Commander (A) N. S. Hanson, RNVR, Commanding Officer of 1833 Squadron, who had eight Corsairs as stern cover for the Avenger force, gives some idea of the trials and tribulations of providing low cover against a determined enemy, even if their attacks might have been better co-ordinated.

'We were too busy on the climb to take much interest in the rest of the escort. Once we levelled out on top, however, I

was a bit shattered to find that our eight Corsairs constituted the whole of low cover. Where the hell were the Fireflies? I hadn't the faintest idea what had happened to them and at this stage was reluctant to break radio silence to find out. We positioned ourselves over the centre of the bomber force and hoped for miracles.

'Quite suddenly there was no more time to goof at the breathtaking scenery. Things began to happen. The Avengers opened the taps, pushed the stick over a little and cracked on more speed. Palembang appeared and, away in the distance, the Banka Strait gleamed in the sunshine with the river, glinting snakelike, winding through the flat country to join it. There, astride the river, lay the massive refinery, a town in itself. I was still taking in the spectacle when —

"RATS!! Eleven o'clock up!!"

'Top cover was shouting the odds and the battle was joined. The air became alive with warning shouts, orders to close up and all the natter that excitement generates. And then I could see them. Over to the North, pinpricks of black were hurtling downhill from a great height and con trails were streaming out across the unbelievably blue sky as our fighters pulled tight corners to get at them. The Avengers were now deploying for their bombing run and their line was lengthening. Christ! I could do with 20 Corsairs right now! Suddenly a Jap levelled out over the port side, going like smoke as he made his run to take the bombers on the beam.

"Break left — GO!"

'The flight wheeled over on to its

wingtips. We gave him a burst head-on and he ducked. Whether or not we hit him I don't know, but fire from 24.5 guns is enough to make the bravest put his head down. I hadn't turned back to the Avengers before someone yelled.

"RATS! Three o'clock up!"

'There were two more, belting downhill at high speed. The other flight had already turned at one of them and we took the other. Someone must have been a damned good shot at three-quarters deflection, for bits and pieces flew off him as he dived down, down — he had forgotten all about the bombers now. We had given him something more to think about! Then we turned back again. The Avengers were now diving steeply on their run to the target. The bloody great balloons were still up, floating between us and the earth like some fat, green, obscene reptiles with red spots. And I cursed the Fireflies. They were the great destroyers who were going to clear these ugly sausages out of the way for us; and as far as I knew their crews were still sitting in their wardroom with their feet up, reading *Lady Chatterley's Lover*. Where the hell were they? We were searching ahead, weaving all the time like maniacs, when tracer tore past us, fired from astern. There in my mirror — he looked as though he were sitting on my elevators — was an Oscar, his guns flashing along his wings. I had time neither to shout nor to break before he dived beneath us, only to re-appear in a split second, pulling up in front of us, the length of two cricket pitches away. We all heaved back on our sticks and gave him the works; no need for gunsights. The silly bastard was half-

stalled, sitting there like a broken-down whore. His port aileron took off and sailed over our heads. What looked like a section of flap fell away to our right. Someone must have hit his engine, for he fell, smoking, down on the port side and Matt Barbour must have nearly flown through him. God knows how he missed him. I yelled and did an aerobatic turn to port where a Tojo was boring in. Business was brisk and we were dashing about like frustrated virgins. I straightened up on the line of the last Avenger or two and looked round quickly to see how the boys were faring. Reggie Shaw and Matt Barbour — Numbers Three and Four — had vanished. I did a quick scan around the local sky — not a sign. How had they gone? Had that Oscar got them? I couldn't remember when I had last seen them. Had that last desperate break thrown them out of formation? When you lose a fast-flying formation, you can be two miles away before you realise it. Whatever the reason, Jimmy Clarke and I were alone. Our other flight had disappeared too. Perhaps they were already on their way to the rendezvous on the far side of the target area. So we pushed off in that direction, diving to get up some more speed.

'Quite suddenly, out of an empty space, rose a Nick — a sleek two-engined fighter. He came up like a rocket on our starboard side and obviously hadn't seen us. I saw quite clearly the two Japs sitting side by side in the greenhouse. Jimmy was the nearer of the two of us and turned to give him a quick squirt. I lifted and horsed the stick over, firing over the top of Jimmy's Corsair. The Jap fell away to starboard, with strikes evident on his port wing; and for one fleeting moment the idea of following him down entered my head. Then I remembered what my job was — it certainly wasn't *that*. A year before I had been reprimanded for forsaking the bombers to shoot up aircraft. I sucked my teeth and flew on to the rendezvous.'

Hanson crashed into the sea half-a-mile astern of his carrier but, although being carried below the surface, unconscious and still strapped in his cockpit, he recovered before his Corsair finally sank, escaped from the aircraft and was picked up by a destroyer some 35 minutes later.

He was a true aficionado of the Corsair. To him, there was no other fighter. He was ready to admit that British aircraft were comparatively without vices at critical speeds, but under operational conditions and at operational speeds, he considered the Corsair to be 'streets ahead.'

The Pladjoe strike was followed on 29 January by an even more successful attack on the Soengei Gerong refinery, also in the Palembang complex. During this strike the Corsair and Hellcat fighters concentrated on the two major airfields. All oil production at the refinery was stopped for two months and, when deliveries started again, they were but a

fraction of the pre-strike output. In addition to 38 aircraft destroyed on the ground by the fighters, over 30 were shot down by the fighter escort.

By this time the British Pacific Fleet had cut the aviation gasoline output from Sumatra to twenty per cent of its normal level, at a time when Japan was desperately short of oil in any form. The effects of the resulting shortage on the campaigns in Burma, on Okinawa, in China and on the Philippines were incalculable, but it is probable that the three strikes of January 1945 were the British Pacific Fleet's greatest contribution to the ultimate defeat of Japan. A few merchant ships were attacked in the course of the strikes. At Pladjoe, one of Japan's largest surviving tankers was damaged beyond repair and enemy aircraft losses to the Corsair and Hellcat fighters amounted to about 140 of all types.

On 23 March, after a short stay in Sydney, the Fleet sailed from the atoll of Ulithi, with orders to keep the Japanese airfields in the Sakishima Gunto islands, halfway between Okinawa and Formosa, out of action during the invasion of Okinawa. There were six airfields on the islands which were in a good position for aircraft bases on Formosa to refuel en route for Okinawa. These fields, too, were ideally situated for the defence of Okinawa.

On 26 March 1945, the first strikes were launched from a position approximately a hundred miles to the south of Sakishima Gunto. Avengers were armed with four 500lb bombs for the purpose of breaking up the runways and destroying hard installations such as hangars, buildings and fuel dumps, while Fireflies used cannons and rockets against the heavy flak emplacements. Corsairs and Hellcats provided escort and target combat air patrol and strafed targets of opportunity, both during and after strikes. On the average, Avenger strikes were flown four times daily. Additional Corsair and Hellcat dive-bombing sorties were flown, so that the enemy was under attack from dawn to dusk.

At the request of the US Navy, who believed that many of the Kamikaze squadrons were based in Northern Formosa, the attack was switched to that island in the early part of April. The carriers were in a launching position on 11 April, but weather conditions caused a delay of twenty-four hours. Even when the striking Avengers and Corsairs did get airborne, a considerable amount of low cloud remained over the airfield targets. A few Corsairs managed to find and attack the airfields in the Shinchiku area, while the Avengers bombed the port of Kirun, inflicting severe damage on the docks, on shipping and on a chemical plant. Later in the day, the Avengers found an airfield and cratered the runways while the Corsairs strafed aircraft on the ground and airfield installations. That evening an enemy attack was detected heading for the Fleet and the Corsair and Hellcat combat air patrol shot down four, damaged six and drove off the remainder before they could reach the ships.

Fleet operations against the Sakishima Group continued until Okinawa was firmly in the hands of the Americans on 25 May 1945; and during that period of no less than 62 days at sea (apart from a break of eight days, spent re-storing and re-arming in Leyte Gulf) was involved in intense operational activity.

After the operations against Formosa, *Illustrious*, badly in need of refitting and with an Air Group which had done more than a full tour of operations, was sailed for the United Kingdom, being replaced by a sister ship *Formidable*, carrying Avengers and Corsair Squadrons 1841 and 1842.

The month of May opened with attacks on Ishigaki. On the 4th, Corsairs and Hellcats accounted for 12 enemy aircraft, including eight Kamikazes. During operations on 4 and 5 May, *Indomitable*, *Victorious* and *Formidable* all suffered attacks by Kamikazes — *Formidable* taking two on consecutive days, with a loss of 29 aircraft — but all three were operational again within a matter of hours.

The 9 May saw more heavy attacks by the suicide squadrons. *Formidable* suffered yet another assault. This time she was caught with her deck congested with aircraft recovered from a recent strike and 18 Avengers and Corsairs were destroyed. Once again she showed her resilience and was operational again within 50 minutes. By this time, however, she was in a situation where she could put only 15 aircraft into the air.

Victorious, too, fell a victim to the onslaught. Two aircraft struck her in quick succession, one exploding near the forward lift, setting fire to the carrier and damaging the lift. The second bounced over the side without exploding, but destroyed four Corsairs in its mad career across the deck.

Nine days later *Formidable* was again a casualty. As a result of an accident, a catastrophic fire engulfed the hangar, set fire to the ship and burned out no less than 30 aircraft. Incredible though it may seem, *Formidable* gallantly weathered the storm again and was once more serviceable by nightfall.

The beginning of June saw the British Pacific Fleet back in Sydney, preparing for the next round — this time, attacks against the mainland of Japan itself. The carrier squadron had changed again. *Indomitable* now undertook a refit and was replaced by *Implacable*. Operations commenced on 17 July 1945 at the height of the typhoon season. The US Navy recalled their first strikes, but Fleet Air Arm Corsairs and Fireflies managed to find and attack airfields and railway yards on the north coast of Honshu.

On 18 July the US Navy attacked the largest Japanese naval base, Yokosuka, in what was regarded as retribution for Pearl Harbor. For what they thought to be political reasons, the British Pacific Fleet was excluded from these strikes and instead was allocated targets to the northeast of Tokyo. As on the previous day, adverse weather prevented all but the Corsairs from reaching the briefed objectives.

On 24 July the US Navy undertook strikes on Kure, while the Fleet Air Arm concentrated on airfields on Shikoku and struck at shipping in the Inland Sea. Light flak was intense around the airfields and losses began to mount, particularly in the Corsair Squadrons. A low cloud base hampered the shipping

strikes, but Avengers, Corsairs and Fireflies found and struck the Japanese escort carrier *Kaiyo*, leaving her on fire and with her back broken. This strike was significant in that it was the only attack made on a Japanese carrier by Royal Navy aircraft.

More shipping strikes followed on 28-30 July. On 28 July, the Inland Sea was again the principal target area, with the important dockyard at Harima being bombed in a dawn strike by Avengers. The naval base at Maizuru, on the north coast of Honshu, was attacked by Corsairs and four destroyer escorts were sunk or damaged badly during the day. A few Japanese aircraft were shot down. Fighter resistance was rare at this point as the Japanese had done an extremely efficient job of dispersing their aircraft in an attempt to conserve their resources for the inevitable Allied amphibious landings. Unfortunately for the enemy, the dispersal was so effective that they found it almost impossible to gather sufficient fighters to meet a threat at any one target. As a result, Allied fighters were rarely called upon to protect the strike aircraft from interference, although the flak remained intense.

On 9 August the weather improved and the Fleet Air Arm enjoyed further success against shipping south of Tokyo and off northern Honshu. Corsairs alternated with Avengers in strikes which kept up continuous pressure against the enemy's dwindling navy and merchant fleet. Small craft suffered most heavily and in Onagawa Wan harbour all the shipping remaining afloat was sunk by the concerted air attacks.

On 9 August Lieutenant R. Hampton Gray, of the Royal Canadian Naval Volunteer Reserve, was leading a formation of 1841 Squadron Corsairs from *Formidable* in a strike on Shiogama. In spite of the intense opposition from shore batteries and ships, Gray pressed home his attack on an enemy escort sloop lying in the harbour of Onagawa Wan and succeeded in sinking it with a direct hit, even though his own aircraft was in flames. Immediately after this attack, his Corsair plunged into the sea and Gray was lost. He was subsequently awarded a posthumous Victoria Cross, only the second to be awarded to a naval aviator in World War II.

On V-J Day there were four Fleet Air Arm carriers at Sydney preparing for operations in the East Indies and the Philippines. These four ships were given the task of re-occupying British territories. HMS *Venerable* and *Indomitable* sailed to Hong Kong, where the two ships launched the last Fleet Air Arm offensive sorties against Japanese forces. On 31 August and 1 September, Corsairs, Hellcats, Avengers and Barracudas dive-bombed and strafed suicide boats which were preparing for a last attack and went on to destroy those that remained hidden in the bays on the north of Hog King Island.

The other task of the carriers was a melancholy one — that of dumping Lend-Lease aircraft into the sea off Sydney. Under the term of the Lend-Lease agreement, aircraft that were retained had to be paid for, or they had to be returned to the United States. The US did not want the aircraft returned and Britain did not want to pay for them, so there was no alternative and the waste was inevitable. A few Corsairs were retained, but these squadrons were decommissioned fairly rapidly. By the end of 1945, only four remained — Nos 1831, 1846, 1850 and 1851. They stayed in service with the post-war Fleet Air Arm until the following summer, when they too were decommissioned.

Top left: FAA Corsair IVs (FG-1Ds) of No 1850 squadron aboard the light fleet carrier HMS *Vengeance* in the Malta area, June 1945.
/*Jim Sullivan.*

Centre left: An FAA Corsair from HMS *Victorious.*
/*US National Archives.*

Bottom left: An FAA Corsair IV (FG-1D) of No 1842 Squadron from HMS *Formidable* aboard the USS *Shangri La* (CVE-38), 21 July 1945./*US National Archives.*

Below: An FAA Corsair IV (FG-1D) landing aboard HMS *Vengeance.*
/*Vought Aircraft via Art Schoeni.*

Night Fighting Corsairs

The possibility of intercepting enemy aircraft at night by means of radar had been brought into sharp focus during the German night blitz on London. Night fighting was a new, highly complex operation which involved not only the aircraft and its crew, but also a controller on the ground, whose task it was to direct the airmen by means of radar to an interception point. There, the plane's own radar could be used to seek out the foe, and its guns to shoot him down.

Although the US Navy had pioneered the use of radio direction finding techniques in the 1920's and early 1930's, the British had made the great advances in the field in the years prior to 1941. It was to the British then that the US turned for guidance, particularly over the use of radar in aircraft. In 1941, many US Army, Navy and Marine Corps officers were sent to Great Britain to learn about Royal Air Force night interception operations. To provide the United States with the capability for more intensive radar research, the National Research Council established, with the assistance of British scientists, the Radiation Laboratory at the Massachusetts Institute of Technology in early 1941.

Shortly after the first flight of the XF4U-1 Corsair, it became obvious to the Navy that the Corsair design had characteristics that would make it suitable for development as a night fighter for both the Navy and the Marine Corps. On 8 November 1941, the Navy forwarded a proposal to Vought to study the design of an F4U-2, which would be an F4U-1 Corsair day fighter adapted as a night interceptor.

At the time of the Japanese attack on

Below: Boresighting the five 50-calibre machine guns in Major Everette H. Vaughan's F4U-2, No 201, at Marine Corps Air Station Cherry Point in late 1943. The guns were boresighted to converge at the aiming point of the radar in the gunsight mode, and then realigned at a slightly different reference point, fore and aft of the boresight centre, to give a slight scattergun effect.
/John Thistlethwaite

Left: F4U2, No 6, which was assigned to VF(N)-75 squadron pilot Lieutenant Junior Grade Arnold E. Downs. White side bars haven't been added yet to the circular blue field and white star under the starboard wing. /*John Hill*

Below: Lieutenant Commander William J. 'Gus' Widhelm, the CO of VF(N)-75 (with shoulder holster) and squadron pilots Lieutenant Hugh D. 'Danny' O'Neill, Jr (far left), and Lieutenant John S. Hill (third from left). Lieutenant Thomas W. Hunt (second from left) was VF(N)-75's Fighter Director Officer. The other two pilots were attached to a US Army P-38 Lightning night fighter squadron that worked with searchlights. The nurse was passing through on a C-47 air evacuation mission./*John Hill*

Pearl Harbour, Vought had completed the initial engineering design of the F4U-2. A full scale mock-up of the airplane was under construction, and a scale model of the F4U-1 equipped with a radar scanner fairing was being prepared for wind tunnel tests. The F4U-2 mock-up was completed and ready for Navy inspection on 28 January 1942, and by 2 March, Vought had scheduled delivery of the first F4U-2 for August 1942.

On 18 April, the Vice Chief of Naval Operations directed the Chief of the Bureau of Aeronautics to establish a night fighter development unit that would be assigned to Naval Air Station Quonset Point, Rhode Island. The purpose of this unit was the development and testing of night fighter equipment and tactics for the Navy and Marine Corps. On 7 May, this unit was officially

designated 'Project Argus', which was later changed to 'Project Affirm'.

By mid-May, a limited amount of F4U-2 developmental flight testing was being carried out by Vought on the XF4U-1 prototype Corsair. But, by the end of May, Vought announced that F4U-2 deliveries would be seriously delayed by the 'congested condition' of the company's engineering department. The company was estimating that the first production F4U-2 could not be delivered before January 1943. On 29 May, a conference was held at the Vought plant to discuss this serious problem.

The Navy had to take immediate action. And on 24 June, the Chief of the Bureau of Aeronautics directed the Naval Aircraft Factory (NAF) to modify the first production F4U-1 to an F4U-2 night fighter. Vought aircraft would furnish preliminary engineering sketches for the modification, and would also co-operate as required with assistance in this modification.

The first production version of the F4U-1 Corsair made its maiden flight on 25 June 1942, the day after the Chief of the

Top left: F4U-2s of VMF(N)-532 preparing to takeoff for Saipan Island from the USS *Windham Bay* (CVE-92), 12 July 1944. */US National Archives*

Top right: Lieutenant John R. Thistlethwaite taking off from the USS *Windham Bay* (CVE-92) in his F4U-2 Corsair 'Cagey Cajun II', bound for Saipan Island, 12 July 1944. His F4U-2 was one of two that VMF(N)-532 converted from raised canopy F4U-1 day fighters on Roi Island, Kwajalein Atoll. */US National Archives*

Above: VMF(N)-532 F4U-2s parked on the engineering line, Roi Island, Kwajalein Atoll, 1944. The two 'raised' canopy F4U-1s in the foreground are being converted to F4U-2s. */John Thistlethwaite*

Right: Major Everette H. Vaughan, CO of VMF(N)-532, in his F4U-2, No 201 'Shirley June', Roi Island, 1944. The raised tail gear, minus arresting hook, was common to most land-based USMC Corsairs. Marines is stencilled on the vertical stablizer instead of the usual US Navy. */USMC*

Below: Lieutenant Paul E. Dolhonde in F4U-2 No 209, en route to Naval Air Station San Diego, California, December 1943. Because of engine trouble he lagged behind the rest of the flight and flew the last leg of the trip on the wing of the transport that was carrying VMF (N)-532's mechanics and spare parts. */John Thistlethwaite*

Bottom: Captain Nathan Bedell, Executive Officer of VMF (N)-532, making a perfect three-point landing in his F4U-2, No 202, on Engebi Island, Eniwetok Atoll, 1944. */John Thistlethwaite*

Bureau of Aeronautics had directed that this airplane would be the first converted to an F4U-2 night interceptor. By the first part of September, it was at the NAF undergoing conversion to the prototype F4U-2, and Vought was directed by the Navy to discontinue development work on the F4U-2 on December 12.

The first F4U-2 conversion was completed by the end of December, and on 7 January 1943, the airplane was flown to Quonset Point where Project Affirm personnel made final adjustments to the radar equipment prior to starting flight tests. F4U-2 flight testing continued at Project Affirm throughout January, and by the end of the month, the airplane's night fighting capabilities had been satisfactorily demonstrated.

Meanwhile, the Navy had made the decision to convert 12 additional F4U-1 airplanes to F4U-2 night fighters at the NAF, and was planning to form a Marine and Navy night fighter squadron with the 12 aircraft. Additional conversions would be authorised if tests on the prototypes were successful. A total of 32 F4U-1 airplanes were eventually converted to F4U-2s during the Corsair night fighter conversion programme; the last airplane was completed in September 1943. Two additional F4U-1s were later converted to F4U-2s by VMF(N)-532 personnel on Roi Island, Kwajalein Atoll. The F4U-2s eventually served in three night fighter squadrons: VMF(N)-532 (Major Everett

Above: A USMC F4U-1 Corsair carrying a 1000lb bomb on a Brewster centre-line bomb rack. */Vought Aircraft via Art Schoeni*

Centre left: A VMF-214 'Black Sheep' Corsair parked on the Torokina Airstrip at Empress Augusta Bay, Bougainville, December 1943. */US Navy via Jim Sullivan*

Below left: A USMC F4U-1 Corsair taxiing on the Torokina Airstrip at Empress Augusta Bay, Bougainville, December 1943. */US Navy via Jim Sullivan*

Left: US Navy Fighter Squadron VF-74 F4U-4 Corsairs, Grumman F9F Panthers and TBM Avengers, and Douglas AD Skyraiders on board the USS *Bon Homme Richard* (CVE-31) off the Korean coast.
/US Navy via Jim Sullivan

Top: A factory fresh USMC AU-1 ground attack version of the Corsair during a company test flight near Dallas, Texas.
/Vought Aircraft via Art Schoeni

Above: A cannon-armed Marine Fighter Squadron VMF-312 'Checkerboard' F4U-4B Corsair in Korea./*Fred Drinkwater*

Above: Corsairs belonging to
Navy Fighter Squadron VF-44
aboard the USS *Boxer* (CVE-21)
off the Korean coast./*Tom Doll*

Right: A Corsair II of the Royal
Navy's Fleet Air Arm.
/*Scale Models Magazine via R. G.
Moulton*

H. Vaughan) and VF(N)-75 (Lieutenant Commander William J. 'Gus' Widhelm), both of which were land based, and VF(N)-101 (Lieutenant Commander Richard E. Harmer), the first US Navy carrier-based night fighter squadron.

The conversion of an F4U-1 Corsair to the F4U-2 night fighter version involved a large number of modifications. The most extensive of these was the installation of the radome and antenna far out on the leading edge of the starboard wing. The outboard starboard 50-calibre machine gun had to be removed to make room for part of the radar equipment. This modification improved the lateral weight distribution, as well. The standard generator was replaced with one that had a higher output, and a small airscoop was mounted on the starboard side of the engine accessory section compartment to supplement the generator's cooling air supply. Flame dampeners were fitted to the engine exhaust system collector outlets for protective purposes. An IFF radar beacon transponder was then installed in the F4U-2s to enable ground radar controllers to determine the friendly or hostile character of their radar targets.

The Corsair's standard HF radio equipment was not well suited for the ground controlled intercept mission, and a VHF radio was installed in the F4U-2s to provide a better air to ground, and air to air communication capability. A radio altimeter system was also installed primarily for use during night carrier landings. Eventually, this system was also to be used during night bombing and strafing missions. The cathode ray tube indicator scope and controls were mounted in the instrument panel directly in front of the pilot. The panel itself was also extensively modified to adapt it better for use in the night fighting environment.

The Navy's First — Night Fighting Squadron Seventy-Five

VF(N)-75, the Navy's first single engine night fighter squadron was commanded by Lieutenant Commander William J. 'Gus' Widhelm, and commissioned at Naval Air Station Quonset Point, Rhode Island, on 1 April 1943.

In May, night fighter training began in Link trainers, and continued until each pilot had 30 hours. Practice interceptions were flown first during the day, and then at night in F4Fs, and F4Us under control of the Ground Control Intercept (GCI) station at Beavertail, on Jamestown Island.

On 1 June, the first of the squadron's six radar-equipped F4U-2s was received from the NAF. The last was delivered on 25 July. On 2 August, the squadron received orders to proceed to Naval Air Station San Diego, California, for overseas duty. Before leaving Quonset Point, the squadron pilots had averaged 15 night hours in the F4U-2s.

The F4U-2s were ferried cross-country, and all of the squadron's equipment and remaining personnel were flown across. on 21 August, the squadron sailed for Munda aboard the cargo ship SS *Melville E. Stone.* They landed at Espiritu Santo, New Hebrides, on 11 September, where the F4U-2s and equipment were unloaded, radar equipment was installed, and the planes were test flown.

The squadron departed for Munda, New Georgia, on 23 September. There, soon after their arrival, the radar test equipment was set up and the plane's radar equipment was checked. The test equipment was first set up in a tent that was not floored or secured, and a considerable amount of trouble was encountered from coral dust in the equipment. Later, a quonset hut was built and the equipment moved into it, and this set up was entirely satisfactory.

Below: F4U-2, No 212, 'Midnite Cocktail', at Kagman Field on Saipan Island, 1944. This airplane was assigned to Lieutenants Charles E. Caniff and Bruce J. Reuter, and was the airplane Captain Howard W. Bollmann was flying the morning of 14 April 1944, when he intercepted and destroyed a Betty bomber off Engebi Island. /*Jim Sullivan*

The squadron's first night patrol was flown on 2 October. The GCI equipment was not operational yet, but the night fighters were kept on station over the base from dusk until dawn on three-hour patrols, hoping to make a search-light interception. The enemy was active during the first part of October, and although many bombers closed to ground radar range, not once did they close to bombing range. The presence of the night fighters probably kept the enemy from making their bombing runs.

During the last two weeks of October, fifteen single plane night raids were made on Munda. Bombs were dropped during two of these raids, and for a number of reasons, not one successful interception was made. In some instances, the night fighters were scrambled too late, and even though the closing bogie was first picked up at a range of 70 miles and at an altitude of 25,000 feet, the night fighter did not have enough time to get into position for the attack. In addition, inexperienced fighter directors failed to put the night fighters into a position where they could make radar contact. (The squadron's fighter directors were not permitted to direct their own planes, because US Army controllers were in charge of GCI at Munda.) This put the pilots at a disadvantage because they were not trained to work with Army controllers. The enemy's evasive tactics included his deception by the use of 'window' (metallised paper, half as long as the wave length of the GCI radar), which gave false returns.

Throughout the first part of November, VF(N)-75s Corsair night fighters flew dusk to dawn patrols which were controlled by the Marine GCI at the north-west tip of Vella Lavella. The squadron provided Task Force cover during the landings on Torokina, and during these operations, control was by both land based GCI and surface craft. Out of seven attempted contacts on the night of 31 October and 1 November, five were made on airborne radar, but the radar equipment failed during the final approach to target. The other two contacts were visual. One was lost; but on the night of 1 November, the other resulted in the first shooting-down for the F4U-2 night fighter.

Lieutenant Hugh D. 'Danny' O'Neill, Jr., the Executive Officer of VF(N)-75 was flying the F4U-2 and reported: "The enemy was picked up by GCI on the northwest tip of Vella Lavella bearing 300 degrees, 15 miles range at 10,000 feet altitude, and my night fighter was vectored to intercept. Airborne radar contact was made at 2½ miles, but was head-on and contact was lost in four seconds. I made a 180 degree turn to port, and when the distance had closed to ¾ mile, a visual contact was obtained, but the enemy was 3,000 feet above me. The enemy changed course and the visual was lost. My night fighter was again vectored to the enemy and a turn was made ½ mile astern of him where a visual was again obtained. I closed, got in a short burst, and set his port engine on fire. Overtaking speed was too great and I overshot. I made a 360 degree turn and again came out astern of the enemy and made another visual and noticed that the port engine had stopped burning. I closed again and fired 160 rounds, and the Betty went down in flames. The exhaust stacks of the Betty were not flame-dampened so visual contact was easy to make at a

Below: Two of VMF(N)-532's F4U-2s parked at Kagman Field on Saipan Island, 1944. */Jim Sullivan*

range of ¾ mile. The Corsair encountered little difficulty in closing on the Betty although the enemy's speed was 180 knots."

On the night of 11 December, O'Neill startled himself by shooting down another Betty, one that he hadn't even seen. "My night fighter was scrambled for an enemy plane which was on a bearing of 180 degrees, at a range of 18 miles and at 1,000 feet. The enemy was reported by PT boats in the vicinity of Metupena Point, and was not observed by any radar at Torokina. I started to climb on a vector of 180 degrees, and when I reached 1,000 feet, at a distance of 12 miles from Torokina, I test fired my guns. PT boats in the vicinity of the enemy saw me fire the guns, and observed a Betty going down in flames. The PTs did not fire at the enemy and reported that the night fighter had shot him down. I reported that I was aided by Superman. This action was also observed from the beach at Torokina by anti-aircraft observers."

The squadron went back on scramble alert duty on 15 November, except that one patrol per night was flown to cover the Task Forces that were on their way to Bougainville. Between 28 November and 10 December, two patrols were flown each night which were controlled by the GCI at Vella Lavella, and by ground search radar on the Torokina Beachhead at Bougainville.

Torokina Field was opened on 10 December, and the VF(N)-75 Corsair night fighters were among the first aircraft to operate there. The squadron was now maintaining their F4U-2s on scramble alert duty at two airfields, Munda and Torokina.

Lieutenant John S. Hill made his first successful interception on the night of 13 December, when he probably destroyed a float plane at Torokina. "I was on night combat air patrol and was vectored to an enemy plane that had been picked up by search radars at Torokina on a bearing of 180 degrees, range 21 miles from Torokina, at 5,000 feet altitude. My F4U-2 was vectored astern of the enemy and airborne radar contact was made at one mile. The enemy was observed to be below and 15 degrees to port on a heading of 120 degrees. I closed, hoping to get a visual contact in the moonlight before airborne radar contact was lost in the ground return along the coast. At about two miles from the coast, two surface indications appeared on the scope, and the original contact was lost at a range of ¼ mile. The surface indications proved to be PTs, which the enemy search plane evidently saw and had gone down to investigate. I was too slow to follow, and after contacting the PTs on the VHF radio, I broke away so that they could open fire. At this point, GCI lost contact with both the enemy and my aircraft because of the low altitude. The enemy failed to fire at the PTs so they could give me no information as to his course. I headed down moon at 2,000 feet and luckily picked up the enemy again on airborne radar as he moved into position to make a run on the PTs. The enemy was at less than 1,000 feet altitude and rapidly closing to attack the PTs. So I closed to 250 yards and opened fire. Airborne radar contact was at once lost, and although the enemy plane did not burn, I feel certain it was destroyed. Neither the PTs nor search radar saw the bogey again after this action. This unidentified float plane had good flame

Below: VMF(N)-532 F4U-2s parked on the engineering line on Roi Island, 1944./*USMC*

Left: F4U-2s of VMF(N)-532's advanced detachment at Engebi Island, 1944.
/Vought Aircraft via Art Schoeni

Below: F4U-2 No 206 of VMF(N)-532 approaching for a landing on the coral runway at Engebi Island, May 1944. At this time the radome was painted the same colours as the wing surfaces. Later, the paint was removed from the radomes to improve radar system reception.
/John Thistlethwaite

damping, which made visual contact impossible with hazy weather conditions.'

Hill then shot down two Rufe float plane fighters on the nights of 15 and 16 December. "I was vectored by the GCI at Torokina and made airborne radar contact at 5,000 feet altitude, bearing 290 degrees, 20 miles from Torokina. My F4U-2 was indicating 170 knots and closing too fast. But I made a visual contact on a single float, low wing monoplane at the same altitude and 100 yards to port, as I overshot. The enemy saw my Corsair's exhaust flames as I throttled back. And as I crossed under the enemy dropping behind to fire, he began a turn to the right. I lost the silhouette of the enemy in my sight and skidded to the left, again picking up the enemy to my right just as he rolled into a tight diving turn to the right. I followed through and gave him a three-second burst and lost the target in the glare of my muzzle flashes."

"My F4U-2 was on patrol under control of GCI at Torokina and was vectored astern of enemy and had airborne radar contact. While closing, my F4U hit the slipstream of the enemy and he changed course 180 degrees. I was again vectored astern of the enemy and had airborne radar contact and closed to 1,000 feet astern. A visual was then made and the enemy was observed to be making shallow

'S' turns. While maintaining visual contact, I closed to within 100 feet unobserved, and opened fire. Incendiaries were seen striking the wings and fuselage of the enemy. A few seconds later, a large sheet of flame was seen below and in front of the enemy cockpit. The enemy plane did not explode but burned and crashed into the water. At the time of contact, the enemy was at 5,000 feet and holding a speed of 150 knots. The enemy had effective flame dampeners, as I saw exhaust flames only when immediately below and within 100 feet. The moon was high and I believe I would not have had a visual contact on a dark night. My airborne radar was working perfectly and I believe I could have used the radar gunsight, had it been necessary.''

The squadron's luck continued and on the night of 19 December, Lieutenant Ruben L. Johns shot down a Rufe. "I was scrambled for an enemy plane which had been picked up by the GCI at Torokina on a bearing of 270 degrees, range of 30 miles, at 8,000 feet altitude. I was vectored and turned one mile astern of the enemy and at ¾ mile I obtained an airborne radar contact. I closed to 500 yards and saw exhaust flames of the enemy directly ahead and 100 feet above. I closed to 100 yards, fired a short burst, and the enemy was observed to go into flames. I remained in the vicinity and saw

the enemy go into the water still burning. The enemy crash was 230 degrees, 15 miles from Torokina. Enemy speed was 140 knots and I had no difficulty in overtaking him. My airborne radar was working perfectly. The enemy was also observed going into the water by personnel on the beach at Torokina.''

Lieutenant Charles L. Penner started out the New Year of 1944 right by shooting down one Val and probably destroying another on 1 January. "My F4U-2 was vectored behind an enemy who was closing on Torokina, but I could not make contact before he was picked up by our searchlights. When the enemy was illuminated, I made a visual contact at four miles and he was turning out to sea, losing altitude fast. I turned to cut him off, and immediately started to close very rapidly. At a range of 250 yards, I opened fire in a level approach with a deflection of about 45 degrees. Only one of my five guns functioned. I crossed right into him and had to pull over to avoid a collision. The enemy continued on down, burst into flames, and hit the water, bearing 255 degrees, seven miles from Torokina. Enemy was at 6,000 feet altitude when visual contact was first made.''

"My Corsair night fighter was scrambled for a bogey that was first picked up by GCI on a bearing of 130 degrees, range 21 miles and closing. The

Above: Lieutenant Joel E. Bonner on the wing of his F4U-2, No 211 'Line Rider' on Tarawa, 1944. The radar indicator scope, with its protective cover in place, is just visible below the gun-sight. Some of the F4U-2s other unique installations are shown clearly in this photograph: the VHF radio whip antenna aft of the cockpit canopy, the special armour plating on the aft section of the cockpit canopy, and the generator airscoop, which is located on the fuselage approximately 3 feet above the leading edge of the wing root. The airplane's upper cowl flaps had not yet been replaced with the fixed skin that helped prevent engine oil from being thrown on the windscreen in flight. */John R. Thistlethwaite*

Above: VMF(N)-532 mechanics adjusting the port outer wing panel Mark 41-2 bomb rack on Lieutenants Joel E. Bonner's and John A. Tuttle's F4U-2, No 211 'Line Rider', 1944.
/*John R. Thistlethwaite*

controller first vectored me on a bearing of 160 degrees, followed by three course changes to port as I continued a climbing turn for the interception. When I reached an altitude of 6,500 feet, GCI gave me a course of 340 degrees and I immediately made airborne radar contact at two miles. The bogey had by then closed to within two miles from Torokina and was illuminated by searchlights. Anti-aircraft batteries opened fire and the bogey made a 180 degree turn to starboard. I cut across the bogey's turn, still in visual contact, closed to one mile, and again made airborne radar contact. The searchlights lost the bogey and I followed on radar. At 1,000 feet range, visual contact was again established. The bogey at this instant must have observed my Corsair as the rear gunner opened fire, and the enemy pilot headed for a large cloud bank. I closed to 750 feet, opened fire and observed flashes in the vicinity of the bogey's fuselage. Damage was hard to determine due to the enemy's return fire. He then went into a steep dive and entered the clouds. I continued to follow on my airborne radar and when the bogey reached an altitude of 1,000 feet, I pulled away to keep from going into the water. Although he did not burn, and was not observed to crash by anyone on the beach,

he was not again picked up by the Torokina radars. I believe the enemy crashed on a bearing of 230 degrees, 10 miles from Torokina."

Lieutenant Johns shot down his second night intruder, a Val, on the night of 13 January. "I was scrambled for an enemy plane which had been picked up by GCI at Torokina on a bearing of 260 degrees, range 15 miles, after he had made a dive-bombing run on Torokina at 5,500 feet altitude. I was vectored astern of the enemy, and at one mile had airborne radar contact and observed that the enemy was below me and that I was closing too fast. I cut the throttle back, and when I did, the enemy observed my exhaust flames and started shooting at me. I immediately had a visual and fired a short burst at 100 yards. The enemy immediately started evasive turns, and I closed and fired a short burst just as he started to dive for the water. He was observed from the beach at Torokina to go down in flames, and flames were observed on the surface of the water for three minutes. I was immediately vectored on to another bogey so I was unable to observe these results. The kill was confirmed by Lieutenant Robert Garrity, and shore batteries up the coast."

Left: Major Everette H. Vaughan, CO of VMF(N)-532, on the wing of his F4U-2, No 201 'Shirley June' 1944. The F4U-2s distinctive flame dampeners are mounted on the engine exhaust outlets under the fuselage aft of the cowl flaps.
/John Thistlethwaite

Below: Lieutenant Edward A. Sovik, VMF(N)-532's operations and radar officer./Edward Sovik

Air Operations Memorandum No. 25
1 April 1944

Night Interceptions in the Solomons

Since the early days of the Solomons campaign, the Japanese have employed night harassing missions by medium and single engine bombers, and by float planes and flying boats as a principal weapon of aerial warfare. To meet their attacks, night fighters were a necessity. It was not until the first radar-equipped PVs and F4U-2s were moved into the Solomons that the defense against Japanese night flying became effective.

A document received from the Intelligence Section, South Pacific Force, sets forth the history of VF(N)-75 which flew F4U-2s from Munda and Torokina for approximately four months. The six pilots attached to the squadron flew 977 hours, about 780 of which were on combat flights, approximately one hour's combat flying per pilot per day every day.

The squadron's early record was discouraging and for two and a half months only one successful interception was made. Early failures are blamed on delayed scrambling of night fighters, inexperienced fighter direction, and on enemy evasive tactics including the use of "window". The experience gained was put to good use, however, and VF(N)-75's

later record is an impressive one. In a five-week period, the squadron shot down five enemy planes and got one probable.

The squadron considers the maximum desirable speed differential between an interceptor and its target to be 20 knots. 'Once you got him on your scope, you ought to be able to slow down and fly formation on the bastard.' The F4U-2 can fly at 95 knots, but owing to the short range of its present scope and occasional inexpert fighter direction, it cannot decelerate quickly enough to avoid overshooting the comparatively slow-moving Japanese planes. The squadron attributes part of its recent success at interception to the tactics of approaching the bogey from a lower altitude, and slowing down by climbing up. The squadron commander suggests the construction of some sort of dive-brakes to be operated by foot-pedals, permitting controlled and rapid deceleration, as in an automobile.

The men of VF(N)-75 continued on scramble alert duty on Munda and Torokina without event until 7 March, when they also started operations at Green Island. On 21 March, the entire squadron was moved back to Torokina Field, and then on 30 April, it was moved to the island of Emirau, where it operated without event until 20 May. On 21 May, the squadron secured flight operations, and by 23 May, had flown its F4U-2s back to Espiritu Santo. Shortly thereafter, VF(N)-75 was bound for the US.

Major Gregory 'Pappy' Boyington, the CO of VMF-214, the Black Sheep Squadron, had this to say about VF(N)-75's tour of duty in the Munda area. "Living had become more normal around old Munda. Even the nights were at last free from Washing Machine Charlie, because an old Navy friend, Commander Gus Widhelm had a squadron of night fighters based at Munda. These night fighters were Corsairs with a large, bulblike fixture on the wing, a radar, and these planes proved to be very effective too.

"Gus and his boys patrolled by night and slept by day. Most of the Nip bombers were being knocked down long before ever getting close enough to us to hear the guns or see the tracers. I found that Gus and I had different problems on our hands, for he chased a dot around on a radar screen within his cockpit, never looking past the instruments, not until the dot that represented a bomber got very close to the centre of the screen.

"He said that they were in no hurry, as we were; they tracked a bomber, checking its speed, enabling a nice slow closing rate where either a miss or a chance of ramming a bomber was highly improbable. With these night fighters, which involved more thinking than action, the nights were cleared so I had more time to rest, and think too."

Below, below right: VF(N)-101 F4U-2s preparing for takeoff on the USS *Enterprise* (CVE-6), 1944./US National Archives

The Marine's First — Night Fighting Squadron Five-Hundred-Thirty-Two

VMF(N)-532, the Marine Corps' first single engine night fighter squadron was commanded by Major Everette H. Vaughan, and was commissioned at Marine Corps Air Station Cherry Point, North Carolina, on 3 April 1943. The squadron's complement of combat aircraft was to consist of twelve (plus three spares) F4U-2 Corsairs. At the time of the squadron's commissioning these aircraft were still undergoing modification at the NAF.

It was not until August that the first completely modified and radar equipped F4U-2 arrived at Cherry Point and the VMF(N)-532 pilots could begin actual night interception training. Although the aircraft had been almost completely modified, a number of minor modifications, adjustments and corrections still remained to be completed. Armour plating had to be installed on the upper aft section of the cockpit canopy. Some difficulty was being experienced in eliminating ignition noise from the VHF radio receiver, and the engines were still throwing an excessive amount of oil on the windscreens during flight. Brakes, voltage regulators and many other accessories required endless hours of trouble-shooting and experimentation before they were operating properly.

By 10 December, the squadron had received its full complement of combat ready F4U-2s. Flight operations were ordered, secured, and last minute preparations were made for the squadron's movement overseas. The men of VMF(N)-532 left Cherry Point for the West Coast on 18 December, and arrived at Naval Air Station San Diego, California, on 24 December. They sailed for Hawaii on 26 December, and arrived on 1 January 1944. Their stay in Hawaii was brief, and on 7 January, the entire squadron was loaded aboard the USS *White Plains* and sailed for the Gilbert Islands. They arrived at Tarawa Atoll on 14 January, and disembarked on Ella Island.

During the months preceding the arrival of VMF(N)-532, Tarawa Atoll had been subjected to periodic night bombing attacks by Japanese bombers presumably based in the Marshall Islands. It was the mission of this squadron to defend the atoll and the ships in the harbour. Based at Mullinix Field on Ella Island, during the first afternoon ashore, the squadron flew test hops in preparation for the first night patrol. During the afternoon's test hops, it was discovered that the ground radar control station was in such a sad state of repair that the possibility of making a successful night interception was considered highly improbable.

On the night of 15 January, the squadron's second night ashore, the island was called to 'red alert'. Enemy

bombers, estimated to be three in number, were picked up by the ground radar installation. At the time, Major Vaughan was in the air on combat air patrol (CAP). He was given several vectors by the ground controller, but information on the target was inadequate. One of the vectors brought him directly over Ella Island, at which time all the anti-aircraft guns in the vicinity started firing. It was later learned that the IFF in his airplane was inoperative, relieving the Ground Defense Command of any criticism. Vaughan was made Air Defense Commander of the island; and among other things, a new system of the night fighter anti-aircraft liaison was put into use to prevent the recurrence of a similar near catastrophe.

On 17 January, the radar installations on Ella Island again detected the approach of enemy aircraft. Captain Nathan Bedell and Lieutenant John Thistlethwaite were in the air on CAP at the time. The ground radar had no information on the bogey and Thistlethwaite was ordered to return to base in order that an attempt might be made to vector Bedell by dead reckoning to the incoming bogey. Because of the limited information furnished by the ground control station, Bedell was unable to make contact with the raider, who dumped his bombs in the lagoon without damaging any ships.

Four nights later, ground radar installations detected the approach of enemy aircraft. This time the radar did have information on the bogey and Bedell and Lieutenant Charles F. Caniff were scrambled for an interception. Bedell was unable to continue the mission because of a supercharger failure. As the bogey closed, Caniff was given several vectors which should have brought him within range of his own radar. He was unable to get a contact and no interception was completed. Again, the raider did no damage to island installations.

On 15 February, the squadron was ordered to send eight F4U-2s to Roi Island, Kwajalein Atoll, Marshall Islands. Major Vaughan led the airplanes which were flown by way of Makin Island. The seven remaining airplanes, led by Captain Bedell, left Tarawa on 23 February, and arrived at Roi the same day.

Night CAPs were carried on at Roi without event until 27 February, when the squadron was ordered to send an echelon to Engebi Island, Eniwetok Atoll. This advanced echelon was maintained at Engebi from 27 February until 11 June,

with the pilots being rotated approximately every ten days. During this period VMF(N)-532 was providing night coverage for four airfields, Roi and Kwajalein on Kwajalein Atoll, and Engebi and Eniwetok on Eniwetok Atoll.

On 8 March, the island of Engebi was subjected to a bombing raid by an estimated force of eight Japanese bombers. Lieutenants George L. Humberd and Richard Pfizenmaier were in the air on routine CAP at the time of the raid. Again, target information, was inadequate, and before the ground controllers could complete an interception, enemy bombs put the radar ground station's VHF radio transmitter out of commission, making further control impossible. The two night fighters, having no contact with the ground control station were ineffective while the enemy bombers proceeded to make repeated bombing and strafing runs on the island. The fighters attempted to make visual contact on the bombers with negative results.

Operations at both bases consisted of nightly CAPs made by two night fighters. During these patrols, practice interceptions were run continually. Every effort was made to improve the technique of night interception and exercises were held during which enemy attacks were simulated as closely as possible. Edward A. Sovik (former pilot, operations and radar officer of VMF(N)-532) flew on many of these night patrols. The following is his vivid description of the F4U-2's radar system and techniques of night interception.

"The indicator scope, which was mounted at the centre of the instrument panel, was about three inches in diameter. The spiral motion of the scanner, which was both transmitter and receiving antenna, was translated on the screen into a rather surprising pattern. A sweep moved vertically up and down the screen as the scanner nodded. A cycle was completed in two seconds; and echo would appear on both the up sweep and down sweep. The sweep was not a straight line but parabolic, and appeared to be a sort of 'necklace' of beads.

"If a target was in range, its echo would appear as two small dots about $3/16$ of an inch apart horizontally left behind on the phosphorescent screen as the sweep passed. Distance was indicated by the vertical position of the dots on the screen; if the target was extremely far away it was at the top of the sceen; as one overtook the target, the blips would move down the screen. At very best, which was rare, one could detect a target as far away as four miles. The transmission pulses were of very short duration of course. If my memory is correct, they lasted two microseconds. This set a limit to the proximity at which a target could be perceived, since if the echo came back while the radar was still transmitting, it would not be picked up; or if the pulse did not break off clean, the reception would be poor. Practically, the signals would usually disappear at 800 to 1000 feet. The interval between them, during which the scanner (which had a parabolic reflector about 10 to 12 inches in diameter) acted as a receiver was, as I recall, about $^2/_{1000}$ of a second.

"If the target was to the right of the line of flight, the pair of dots would be to the screen's right; and if to the left, to the screen's left. If the target was above the axis of the plane, the right hand dot would be above the left dot by as much as about $^1/_8$ or $^3/_{16}$ of an inch; if the target was below, the right hand dot would be below the left hand one.

"To make a good interception, one would first turn to bring the echo to the vertical centre line of the screen and climb or descend to bring the two dots down to the bottom of the screen by overtaking the target. When the aircraft was directly in line with the target, the pilot could switch the pattern to the gunsight mode. The image then was a dot with lines extending out equally from both sides. If this image was kept centred in the screen, it would grow in size as the aircraft approached the target. A point when it was about $^3/_4$ inch across was supposed to be the firing range. We made no use of this mode because of the danger of attacking a friendly airplane.

"The final approach to the target was critical since it was obviously necessary to avoid becoming a sitting duck to the tail gunner. The rate of approach had to be such that one didn't overshoot, and such that one didn't need to throttle back quickly to avoid overshooting. Our planes were equipped with flame dampeners, which were special extensions to the exhaust pipes, so that under proper conditions the exhaust flares couldn't be seen. But if one throttled back suddenly, the exhausts would flare and there was danger of being seen.

"One also paid attention to the relative brightness of sky, ocean and clouds — particularly on moonlit nights — while planning the final approach, so that the target would be silhouetted and the fighter would not be.

"Since vision at night takes perhaps forty minutes to reach its peak, and since red light does not deleteriously affect night vision, it was our practice to wear red goggles for an hour or so before going on patrol. All the cockpit lighting was red except the scope, and we kept the gain down as low as we could effectively use it. We used oxygen from the ground up, because oxygen is an aid to night vision. And we learned also to search the sky, once we left the radar scope, by looking not directly where we thought the target would be, but 15 to 20 degrees away, since the periphery of the retina is more sensitive to dim shadows than its centre.

"Most of our patrols were at about 20,000 feet, but we sometimes waited at altitudes as high as 28,000, which could be very chilly. The patrols were normally scheduled for two hours, with enough overlap so that two planes were at altitude during the periods of duty. We worked a sort of haphazard schedule depending on a variety of things — weather, condition of plane, radar and pilots — so our lives were pretty irregular. But they had their idyllic aspects. Plenty of sun, water, leisure. And the beauty of the nights was only eclipsed by the glory of the last patrol, when one would frequently see the sun come up and turn the clouds into fire; the clouds would be below, not above, and these occasions were spectacular."

On the night of 13/14 April, pilots of VFM(N)-532 made the Marines' first successful interception in the F4U-2 Corsair. In this action, they intercepted a flight of an estimated number of 12 Betty bombers attempting a raid on Engebi, and shot down two, probably destroyed a third, and routed the rest. All the enemy bombs fell in the ocean.

During this night's operation, Lieutenant Edward A. Sovik was able to climb his F4U-2 to 20,000 feet in ten minutes. He was then vectored on to a bogey. He made visual contact, identified the aircraft as enemy, and within fourteen minutes after takeoff, had fired at it and had seen it explode. Captain Howard W. Bollmann also successfully intercepted and shot down one of the enemy bombers, and then almost collided with it. Lieutenant Joel E. Bonner, Jr., was not so fortunate. Although the bomber he intercepted was listed as a 'probable', it nevertheless damaged his F4U-2 so badly that he was forced to bail out. A destroyer rescued him late in the afternoon of the next day. Lieutenant Frank C. Lang completed several

Above: An F4U-2 of VF (N)-101 getting the takeoff signal on board the USS *Enterprise* (CVE-6), 1944.
/Vought Aircraft via Art Schoeni

interceptions, but all of his targets turned out to be radar confusing 'window', which the bombers had thrown out on their way in.

Lieutenant Donald Spatz was lost during this action. At the first sign of the incoming raid, Spatz was scrambled and turned over to the control of a Navy shore-based fighter director unit based on Eniwetok. Out of the melee of planes and window, a plane emerged which the controller erroneously believed to be Spatz, even through its position was not consistent with the dead reckoning plot. Spatz was given a vector to bring him back to the base, and consequently he was led out of control range and became lost.

The following are official accounts of the three Marine Corps pilots who scored victories in their F4U-2 Corsairs that night in April. Lt Joel E. Bonner was the first to engage the enemy and reported:

"I took off for regular CAP at 2400. At the time of takeoff, the ground station had one plot on what turned out to be a bogey.

After giving 'airborne', I was given, 'Vector, 230 degrees, angels 10'. About the time of attaining angels 10, I was given, 'angels 20, climb fast'. This was my first indication that something was up. At angels 15, GCI instructed me to orbit port and continue to climb.

"I judge at this time Lieutenant Donald Spatz was airborne. However, I did not hear the transmission turning Lieutenant Spatz over to the Argus unit at Eniwetok.

"Nearing angels 20, GCI gave information on bogey as coming toward me heading for the atoll. Bogie's altitude was 20,000; speed 120. Immediately following this information, I was given a safety vector of about 090 degrees and shortly after that I was given an on course of 050 degrees, range 3 miles.

"At 0034 I got a contact at range 2½. Angels were the same. At this time the moon was a few degrees above the horizon. It was slightly over half full.

"All this time the controller showed very little emotion which put some doubt in my mind as to the bogey. However,

upon getting the contact this doubt was extinguished. I immediately charged my guns, turned on the gun sight to proper intensity, turned all gun switches on, and left the master gun switch off.

"I closed with the bogey finding his altitude and speed that which the ground station had given me. I closed with my signals showing five to ten degrees to the starboard. Obtained visual from search range approximately 1,200 feet. The position of the moon was to the starboard. Noticing very few clouds, I closed on up from directly astern. I gave 'Tallyho', a description of the bogey, and noticed that I was opening fire, for GCI acknowledged, 'go to it'. My range was point blank; the target completely filling and over-lapping the gun sight. I opened fire; only my starboard two guns fired. Upon realising this, I recharged my left wing guns. As all five guns commenced firing, the tail gunner of the Betty let go at me. He got a short burst into me before his ship dropped its starboard wing and started down. I tried to follow only to get a large amount of oil on the windscreen.

"I informed GCI I was hit and asked for a steer to base. 060 degrees was the steer given, with range 12. GCI inquired if I could make it inside the bounds of the atoll. I tried adding throttle but that had no effect. I informed GCI that at 6,000 feet I was getting out. At 6,000 feet I called up and said I was unhooking and going over the side. I allowed the plane to slow down as slow as possible and went out the port side, diving out and down.

"When free in the air I pulled my rip cord. Everything went fine. I wasn't able to get my leg straps through the seat pack, but was clear of the chute, so it was simple to pull in the pack and free it of the leg straps.

"The raft inflated easily and I crawled aboard, only to find myself with flutters in the stomach from the excitement. This must have been around 0045. I saw from the raft what I learned later was Captain Bollmann's Betty burst into flame and go down.

"It was pretty cold that night and the opposite the next day. I could see the destroyer escort (DE) that night

Above: A VF(N)-101 F4U-2 being raised from the hangar deck of the USS *Enterprise* (CVE-6) on the No 2 elevator, 20 January 1944.
/*US National Archives*

searching, and the searchlights on Eniwetok. The next morning I saw numerous planes before I was sighted by a B-25 only to be lost again. I wasn't sighted again until around 1600 in the afternoon, when the same B-25 found me. The rescue was accomplished by the DE. A small boat can really look large, when desired."

Lt. Edward A. Sovik made the second interception and described his mission:

"Radar contact with the first bogey was made shortly after 2400, 13 April 1944, by SCR-270s. The bogey was at about 83 nautical miles distance, and Lieutenant Joel E. Bonner in plane 215 was vectored to intercept him. Word was sent to scramble two more fighters besides the one in the air. Lieutenant Donald Spatz took off about 0025 in 208. Lieutenant Frank C. Lang followed him in 207. Another fighter was requested, and Captain Howard W. Bollman scrambled in 212 about 0045. Lieutenant Bonner having made contact, was shot down and was parachuting about this time, and a fifth fighter was requested.

"The remaining plane with functioning AI was 202. This plane had been grounded by the previous pilot, because of lack of VHF reception and because the secondary channel was very noisy. The faulty VHF had been traced to a faulty solder connection in the control box cable, and it was torn apart and under repair at the time the plane was scrambled. I arranged the radio cords so that the VHF could be used, had good communications on the deck and took off at about 0030.

"GCI instructed me to vector 270, climb as fast as possible to 16,000 and orbit about 10 miles west of base. While I was climbing, the altitude instructions were altered to 20,000. Shortly before this altitude was reached, a new vector of 230 was given with a reminder to orbit 10-12 miles from base. During the last part of the climb, the radio became extremely noisy with interference of many varieties, music, garbled voices, singing and plain noise, so that the last lucid transmission received from Razor Base was the question, "What are your angels?' They were 20, and it was almost precisely 10 minutes after takeoff. Then I began orbiting.

"On the way up, I had charged my guns but had not fired them, not wanting to display the flashes while heading west. I had turned on my gunsight also, and adjusted it to a suitable intensity, and had started AI in operation. It appeared to be functioning well.

"While heading generally west in my orbit, I noticed a signal appeared about 2½ miles out and at nearly extreme azimuth. I deepened my left turn to bring the target in farther and soon discovered that the target was above and on an opposite course. The echoes were excellent, so that I was never uncertain of them.

"I had gotten the impression, supposing that I was the fifth man in the air, that I would not be used as a fighter, but would be kept orbiting as a reserve, or merely to keep the plane off the deck and out of danger of bombing. Since nothing had been told me during the climb of any approaching bogey, this impression had been strengthened. So when I saw the echo it appeared that this was probably a friendly plane. I called Razor Base repeatedly requesting information, hoping that some word might get through. But except for once near the end of the chase, when word came uncertainly to 'go ahead and fire', communications were impossible.

"I followed the target, nevertheless, meaning to identify it before shooting and prepared myself, except for leaving the individual gun switches off, for the attack. The approach was normal and I observed the target's course to be about 080 magnetic. At 23,000 feet I hit a slipstream and dropped down slightly, throttling back, I did not switch to gunsight position at all, but brought the target down close to about 10 to 15 degrees to the starboard.

"This seemed a sound approach, since the moon was about 15 degrees up and the eastern sky was bright. It proved to be so, for at first glance away from the scope I saw the target clearly silhouetted about 300 yards away. Scrutiny made it unmistakably a Betty.

"I turned to bring him in my sight and abruptly hit the very turbulent slipstream. The F4U stalled, went off on its wing with a jolt and lost about three or four hundred feet before I could begin to bring the nose up. Aside from being startled, I was very apprehensive, first lest the rear gunner see me against the light clouds below, and also lest I lose my visual. Fortunately neither occurred, and when I recovered from the stall I was in a good position to start a run. The 300 yards had shrunk to about 200, and as I pulled up the rate of closure fell.

"I got the target in the sight, pushed the gun switches all together (missing two of them) and fired a series of short bursts in quick succession, pausing between them only long enough to notice what damage was done. The target was slightly to the starboard to begin with, the port engine was the most obvious target. It began to smoke a little after the first burst. A couple of subsequent bursts seemed to be starting fires in the wing roots, but they blew out. By this time I had swung almost astern and the starboard engine was a good target. I gave it a burst and paused to note that smoke was coming thickly from each engine and the plane was in a nose down glide. I got on again now at a range of about 125 yards and fired a last burst, the longest. The plane suddenly burst into a bright streak of flame. I followed him, burning more and more brightly, down to 20,000 feet. Then I levelled off. Some lesser flashes, and one very bright one visible through the window at the bottom of the cockpit, gave evidence of an explosion. I turned on my wing and saw the remains disappear glowing red in the water.

"When the Betty was burning, I called Razor Base and informed them. Getting near the base (I was then perhaps 7 to 8 miles out) seemed to improve communications; and I heard them say there had been another plane shot down. Looking south I saw another stream of fire. Captain Bollmann's plane.

"Razor Base instructed me to orbit, so I climbed to 22,000 and orbited. Again incommunicado, I discovered that I had only used three guns. Ordnance crewmen subsequently observed an absence of less than 100 rounds.

"Aside from communications, all went well. The AI performed excellently and continued to do so for at least 1½ hours more continuous operation, during which time I was hoping to encounter another target. The gunsight was excellent. The loading satisfied me, and I was surprised that I could see where I was hitting by dim white flashes — apparently the incendiaries. The performance of the plane was irreproachable."

Captain Howard W. Bollmann reported:

"I had just returned to my tent after flying CAP from 2100-2400 and was getting ready to hit the sack when the command car driver came to pick up Lieutenant Frank C. Lang. He told me that there was to be an alert so I rode to the line with Lieutenant Lang, not intending to fly but to help out on the ground. As we arrived at the line, Lieutenant Donald Spatz took off (0025) and Lieutenant Lang took off shortly afterward. I stood by the phone as Lieutenant Edward A. Sovik, the duty officer was busy elsewhere. About this time, the sirens sounded and about 0038 the phone rang, requesting another fighter. I ran out and scrambled in F4U-2 No. 212 at about 0045, just in time to hear Lieutenant Joel E. Bonner announce that he was ready to jump. Tested guns immediately after takeoff; all okay, so I kept on all switches but master gun.

"I was vectored 270 degrees to angels 20. When I had reached twenty miles from base, I orbited once in my climb and reached angels 20 immediately (12 minutes after takeoff). As soon as I reported 'level' I was given a customer, vector 260 degrees. Approximately one minute later, I picked up a contact at three and one half miles ahead. It soon became obvious that we were on opposite courses, and at about two miles I commenced a hard starboard 180 degree turn, informing controllers of my actions. I turned a bit past 180 degrees (to 100 degrees), to get back on my original track and immediately picked up the bogey at two and one half miles, azimuth 30 left above; turned astern of target on course 080 degrees. Informed controllers I still had contact and they relieved themselves of me, as they had two more fighters to watch. Closed rapidly to half mile while climbing to target's angels of 22. At half mile I slowed to speed of target to plan my attack. There was a white cloud base below, and I had no desire to be seen against it. (The moon was between one and two o'clock and 15-20 degrees elevation). I played with the idea of getting above the target so as to see him against the clouds. But I was afraid he might be lost under a wing or nose of my plane, so I decided to come in at targets angels and 5 or 10 degrees on my down moon side of target, (port side). After checking my gun switches I added speed and crept up on target, as I was 10 degrees off target. Sight position was inoperative, and I used search all the way, and at 300 yards I looked up and saw the target exactly where he should have been. I immediately speeded up and closed very rapidly; opened fire at 150 feet dead astern and 15 feet below aiming at right wing root. I was startled by lack of tracers — had the feeling that my bullets were going astray — and fired less than two seconds. The starboard engine was smoking. I then transferred aim to port and after another two second burst observed flame and smoke on port engine. (At first I mistook white flashes from my

Right: The USS *Enterprise's* (CVE-6) F4U-2 Night Fighter Team. Standing, L to R: Poirer, Brunson, Harmer, Orphanides (Radar Technician), Rowlen; Kneeling, L to R: Holden, Kelly, Von Specken./*Richard Harmer*

Below: A VF(N)-101 F4U-2 with a catapult bridle attached just prior to a catapult launch off the USS *Enterprise* (CVE-6), 1944. The radio altimeter transmitting and receiving antennae are clearly visible on the bottom of the fuselage.
/*US National Archives*

incendiaries to be return fire and instinctively ducked behind my engine; however, at no time did I receive return fire — those babies didn't know what hit them.) By this time the target was in a 15 degree nose down attitude and I dang near rammed him. Employing what might be termed an outside snap roll to avoid him, I pulled around to one side and above to observe the plane. From this position it appeared that the flame had blown out, so I gave him another short burst from 20 degrees above and astern 100 yards. Fifteen seconds later he broke into two pieces and dropped to earth in flames. At the time of explosion, lights, which might have been flares or 'gizmos' dropped from the plane. I looked at my watch — it was about 0110, 20 minutes after takeoff. Spent the next two hours orbiting, as the SCR-527 was out of commission due to vibrations from the AA guns. I kept my AI on for about one hour in the hope of picking up another target.

"The AI was working well, except that it had to be tuned manually. Guns functioned perfectly. Used about sixty rounds of each; I would like to suggest testing one tracer in each 10 or 15 rounds in two of the guns. It gave me a funny feeling to shoot and not see my bullets going into the target. During the latter part of the two hours Lieutenant Frank C. Lang and myself endeavoured to locate Lieutenant Donald Spatz to no avail."

On 11 June, the advanced detachment at Engebi rejoined the rest of the squadron at Roi Island, and from that date to 29 June, VMF(N)-532 carried on routine CAPs in defence of Kwajalein Atoll.

On 19 July, the squadron commenced night CAP operations over Guam Island. These patrols were carried on without event until 4 August, when the squadron was ordered to start flying bombing and strafing missions against airfield installations on Rota Island during the flight to and from Guam. En route to Guam, the airplanes bombed the airfield installations, and on the return trip, made a single strafing pass. The squadron flew these missions nightly through 7 August.

Air Operations Memorandum No. 39
16 July 1944
Night Bombing by F4Us
Early reports from VMF(N)-532 indicate that a new hazard has come to the Japanese in the Marshalls. From 30 June, through 2 July, this night fighter squadron conducted six night bombing and strafing missions over Wotje for a total of 28 sorties. The Corsairs each carried two 250lb general purpose bombs and flew toward the target at 6,000 to 8,000 feet. Altitude was lost during the approach, until the planes were at 3,500 to 4,500 feet. With one exception, dives were made singly, and only one bomb was released on each dive. Diving speeds averaged 250 knots; and the dive angle varied from 20 to 60 degrees with 45 degrees the most usual; and altitude of release averaged 1,400 feet. Bombing runs were followed by strafing runs, with the result that on the three nights there were a total of about 50 separate attacks; 28 bombs were released with 24 hits in the target area, and 4,500 rounds of 50-calibre ammunition were expended.

The squadron resumed night CAP operations over Saipan on 8 August, and continued flying these missions without event until 20 September. On 21 September, the squadron was ordered to secure flight operations and prepare to return to the US. The F4U-2s were all flown to Guam Island for further transfer, and by 23 September, the pilots were aboard an air transport bound for the US.

The First Carrier Based-Night Fighting Squadron One-Hundred-One
Commander Richard E. Harmer was Commanding Officer of the first US Navy carrier-based night fighter squadron,

VF(N)-101. This squadron originally was part of VF(N)-75 which was commissioned at Naval Air Station Quonset Point, Rhode Island, in April 1943. In the summer of 1943, six experienced pilots of VF(N)-75 were sent to operate from land bases in the Pacific, and the rest, under Harmer, remained at Quonset as the second unit of VF(N)-75. Ultimately, in January 1944, this unit was commissioned as VF(N)-101, and all of its carrier duty was as squadron VF(N)-101. Harmer discusses in detail combat experiences of his squadron, which was the first carrier-based US Navy Corsair Squadron.

"This discussion concerns itself with the seven man, four plane team which was aboard the USS *Enterprise*. We went aboard ship 16 January 1944, and shoved off for a six month cruise, during which we went through the Marshals landing, raids on Truk, Hollandia, Palau, and finally the Marianas landing. We returned to the United States 22 July 1944, where the squadron was disbanded and the personnel assigned other duties.

"The squadron had a record of five Japanese planes destroyed, and two damaged in night actions. I believe that our work, together with that of other night fighter carrier-based squadrons, has demonstrated the need for an abundance of well trained night fighter pilots who can carry on a variety of missions against sea or land targets. Our squadron had only limited opportunites. We had ten night contacts and engaged in numerous rescue missions and searches for lost planes. But the whole field of intruder work, night bombing by radar-equipped planes, and large scale night interceptions were types of missions not available to us. I am sure that these and other missions could be performed very well by carrier-based night fighters. During our tour of duty we averaged about ten hours flying per month per pilot. Most of this was during the daylight on such missions as leading 0S2U Kingfisher rescue planes to downed pilots. On one occasion, we flew CAP over the troop transports from 0415 until sunrise, when we were relieved by a day fighter CAP.

"Our first real contact resulted in a 'probable'. This came early in the morning of 19 February, when our force was off Truk. This 'probable' could have been turned into a kill, except that the fighter director brought his plane in above the bogey and the pilot overshot on two occasions. When visual contact was finally obtained, a red glow was noticed immediately aft of the right engine, following a short burst, but contact was lost as the target appeared to be going in a steep spiral. The pilot failed to place his target on visual before opening fire and had dropped so far back he lost visual contact after the fire went out.

"More than two months passed before we got another chance. This time the results were more favourable. Contact was established on radar (after several radical changes of vectors) at two miles range, 30 degrees to port. Visual contacts were established by both planes; the tail gunner opened fire on me at 250 yards. After once losing contact, I regained it on the scope and closed to about 300 yards at which position both the tail and dorsal gunners fired at me. I slid back on his tail and gave him another long burst at less than 150 yards; and after another "S" turn to reduce speed, I closed in again until I was close behind him and at less than 100 feet altitude. He was flying so low that the propwash foamed the water. Consequently, I had to depress my nose in order to hit the target. Anyhow, he finally went down after I had used 950 rounds.

"That expenditure was unfortunate because a few minutes later I ran into the chance of a lifetime, a Jap bomber formation flying at night with lights on. The indications on the scope showed the presence of at least five targets, but only three seemed to be showing lights. The faulty ammunition was to let me down again, because the guns worked for only half a second and then stopped. The plane I fired at dropped his left wing and flashed a row of four vari-coloured lights along the upper surface or each wing. The other two planes followed suit. A little later, I got one gun working and as soon as I had fired three rounds, it stopped. The plane I fired on turned on his vari-coloured lights and the whole formation again followed suit. I never did figure out what those lights were for, unless they thought I was a friendly plane trying to join up on them and they were trying to identify themselves. I believe that the plane I had knocked down was their "snooper", and they thought I was he returning to formation.

"Nearly two months passed before we had another real chance. That time, Lieutenant Junior Grade R. F. Holden, Jr. and I ran into a large formation of two-engine planes escorted by a flight of Tojos. Holden knocked one off my tail and it disappeared from view at 1,500 feet, headed down in a tight spin. It was rated as another possible.

"Little more than a week later we hit the jackpot. As a raid was approaching the task group, Holden was catapulted. He went off on the vector immediately and climbed to 10,000 feet, established contact and was ready to fire all within 10 minutes. He was none too fast, either, because just as the break-off order was going to be passed (he and the bogey were approaching the Task Force), we could see his tracers going into the Jap plane, which fell in flames in the midst of the fleet. That put us back in the good graces of everyone and set the stage for the next night when we had a record evening.

"Once again, Holden was catapulted and established a contact at 1,000 feet altitude. The range was three miles, and he closed until he had a visual at 800 feet. He closed to 200 feet dead astern and fired a short burst, hitting the starboard wing stub. The Betty blew up with such a terrific explosion that Holden could feel the heat from the flames. A short time later he was given another vector to a low-flying bogey, and after a long chase, he watched his incendiaries hit the Betty, which burned fiercely as soon as it hit the water. One very important feature of this kill was that the Betty obviously knew Holden was around, and although it took radical evasive action, it was unable to get away from his radar and visual contacts.

"But the night was not over. I was sent off to run a practice interception on Holden as he returned toward the task group. After the practice was over, we joined up and were coming home when the fighter director told us another plane was in our formation. The other plane, of course, was another bogey. I was sent after it, closing on a radar contact to half a mile. I dropped down to 500 feet (he seemed to be at 900) and side stepped to the down-moon side of the target. I continued to close in, all of this time being on radar, until I made a visual at 400 feet range. After slowing down, I pulled up to the target and sent a half-to-one-second burst into the port wing root. The plane exploded immediately and hit the water.

"These three kills in one night came toward the end of June, and shortly afterward we headed toward home. On the way, we had our last contact. Two of our planes were sent after some high-flying Japs, but unfortunately we had at that time the only radar failures of the entire trip. A fleeting visual contact was established by means of expert GCI, but it was not sufficient for the kill."

Corsairs with the Royal New Zealand Air Force

At the time of the Japanese attack on Pearl Harbour in December 1941, the Royal New Zealand Air Force had only one combat fighter squadron, which was in Malaya flying Brewster Buffalos. Relying exclusively on American aircraft to equip its combat squadrons, the RNZAF soon grew into an effective fighting force, and at peak strength had thirteen Corsair-equipped fighter squadrons.

The first deliveries of Corsairs to the RNZAF began on 29 March 1944, and between that date and 15 June 1945, 424 airplanes were delivered. This total was made up of 237 Vought F4U-1s, 127 F4U-1Ds, and 60 Goodyear FG-1Ds. The FG-1Ds did not see wartime service with the RNZAF, but No 14 Squadron was equipped with these aircraft when it served later in Japan as part of the Occupation Forces from March 1946, to November 1948.

The first of the RNZAF Corsairs were shipped directly from the west coast of the US to the island of Espiritu Santo in the New Hebrides. A Corsair Assembly Unit was responsible for assembling the aircraft as they arrived. A Test and Dispatch Flight, under the command of Flight Lieutenant D. A. Grieg, test flew the aircraft as they were assembled and undertook the conversion training of the fighter pilots arriving from New Zealand. By the end of July 1944, there were enough Corsairs available to send some to New Zealand for training, and thereafter, all Corsair transition training was completed there. Corsair assembly was discontinued at Espiritu Santo in December 1944, and the Corsair Assembly Unit was transferred to Los Negros on Manus Island.

As the South Pacific campaign was drawing to a close, the future of the RNZAF became the subject of

Below: The first Royal New Zealand Air Force (RNZAF) F4U-1 (NZ5201) taking off from Espiritu Santo, in the New Hebrides Group, March 1944./*John Regan*

Above: RNZAF F4U-1s of No 18
Squadron flying off the coast of
Guadalcanal, in the Solomon
Islands, March 1945.
/Vought Aircraft via Art Schoeni

Left: An RNZAF Corsair loaded
with a 500lb stick bomb on
Bougainville./*d'E. C. Darby*

considerable discussion between New Zealand and the United States. As early as March 1944, it had been suggested that since there was no longer any Japanese fighter opposition in that theatre of action, there was no point in continuing to send RNZAF fighter squadrons to the forward area. However, in May 1944, it was finally agreed that New Zealand fighter squadrons should continue offensive operations in the Northern Solomons until the Japanese were finally cleared from the islands, even though the aircraft would be employed as fighter-bombers.

During October, November, and December 1944, US Army units were gradually withdrawn from the South Pacific area in preparation for operations in the Philippines, and their place was taken by Australians. Control of land operations on Bougainville was taken over from the US by the 2nd Australian Army Corps on 22 November, and all squadrons of the 1st Marine Air Wing discontinued operations there on December 8. Flight operations on Bougainville were subsequently carried out by the Royal Australian Air Force and RNZAF.

The first RNZAF Corsair unit to enter the combat area was No 20 Squadron, commanded by Squadron Leader S. R. Duncan, which arrived at Bougainville on 14 May 1944. The squadron had been formed at Ardmore, New Zealand, in January, and trained there until April, when it moved to Espiritu Santo. After conversion flying was completed, the squadron flew to Guadalcanal, where it

spent several weeks training before going on to Bougainville.

The terrain on Bougainville was covered with dense jungle, and the enemy took full advantage of the concealment it offered. Targets were extremely difficult to locate from the air, and a lead-in aircraft was normally used to identify them, with smoke bombs. This was usually the task of Boomerangs or Wirraways of the RAAF's No 5 Tactical Reconnaissance Squadron. When the intensity of ground fire made it dangerous for the relatively slow reconnaissance aircraft, a Corsair flown by an experienced pilot was used. Having observed the fall of his bombs, the lead-in pilot, known as "Smokey Joe", orbited the area and told the fighter-bomber aircraft where to drop their bombs in relation to the smoke marker. In close-support operations, targets were frequently marked by ground forces with mortar fire.

The normal bomb load carried by the RNZAF Corsairs was 1,000lbs. The type of bombs used varied with the nature of the target, but this was more often dictated by the supplies available. General purpose bombs were most commonly used, but when they were employed against troop positions,

particularly in swampy areas, they were modified by mounting a 2.5-ft long stick to the detonator. These bombs burst on impact, but made no crater, and produced a very strong lateral blast which destroyed all ground cover in the vicinity of the explosion. Similar results could also be achieved with depth charges.

The campaign on Bougainville assumed a more positive character after the US was relieved by the Australians. The island itself had not been an objective for the US, but a stepping stone in the advance northward, and their land operations were limited there to ensuring the integrity of the airfields at Empress Augusta Bay. The task of the 2nd Australian Corps, on the other hand, was the reconquest of Bougainville.

The first action fought by Australian troops on Bougainville was to capture Pearl Ridge and establish defensive positions there to prevent any further enemy attack on the airfields from the east. Several times during these operations, RNZAF Corsairs gave close air support to the infantry, a role which was to become increasingly more

important in the months to come. On 7 December, eight aircraft of No 15 Squadron, led by Squadron Leader D. P. Winstone, attacked a Japanese position that was holding up troops in their advance from Piaterapaia. The objective was a group of five huts, dispersed over an area of fifty square yards on top of a hill. The Corsairs were led in by two Boomerangs of No 5 Tactical Reconnaissance Squadron. The Boomerangs marked the target by strafing it, and the Corsairs dived down and dropped 325lb depth charges from

Below: An RNZAF Corsair of the No 4 Operational Training Unit at Ohakea, New Zealand, 1945. /*John Regan*

800 feet. Depth charges had not been used against land targets on Bougainville up to this time, but experience by Royal Air Force squadrons in Burma had shown that they were ideal for jungle bombing.

Another strike was made in the same region the following week. The Australians were to attack Japanese troops entrenched on a hillside half a mile south of Retsiopaia, and eight Corsairs of No 15 Squadron, each carrying a depth charge or a 500lb bomb, went in first to soften up the position.

The year 1945 started with two New Zealand fighter squadrons, Nos 21 and 24 stationed on Bougainville. They were relieved in January and February by Nos 18 and 20, both of which remained on the island until April. By April, there was no longer a requirement to provide fighter squadrons for garrison duty in the South Pacific area, and squadrons coming from New Zealand went straight to the forward area instead of being held for duty at Espritu Santo or Guadalcanal. It was then possible to increase the number of RNZAF Corsair squadrons operating on Bougainville to four. At the beginning of May, Nos 14, 16, 22, and 26 squadrons were stationed there, all of which had arrived during April. They were relieved in June and July by Nos 15, 18, 23, and 24, the four fighter squadrons that were on Bougainville when the war ended.

The RNZAF Corsair squadrons were based on the Piva Airfields, and were responsible for flying dawn and dusk patrols over the Empress Augusta Bay area in the unlikely event that Japanese aircraft ventured into the region. Their primary mission, however, was to make bombing and strafing attacks on Japanese positions on Bougainville. The aircraft also flew daily along the coast of the island, searching for Japanese in canoes and other small craft.

Twelve Corsairs, on fifteen-minute alert, were kept at the disposal of the forward brigade in southwest Bougainville. Field Headquarters at Piva was in direct contact with the forward command, who called for strikes, provided target information, and arranged to have the targets marked.

During the first three months of 1945, when two fighter squadrons were based at Piva, the RNZAF Corsair daily sortie rate ranged from eight to forty-six, depending on the weather, the number of aircraft available, and operational requirements. A normal day's effort consisted of about thirty sorties. In April, with four squadrons available, the number of attacks rose sharply, and the daily sortie

rate averaged between fifty and sixty. During the next three months, the average rose even higher, and at times, aircraft from Green Island had to be called in to lend their support. On special occasions, over a hundred sorties were flown in a day.

Before the Australians began their move forward from the Jaba River line in January, RNZAF Corsairs were used to soften up Japanese positions and interrupt communications in areas immediately to the south. When the offensive got moving after the middle of January, ground and air operations became progressively more integrated. Strikes behind the Japanese lines were ordered as part of the general preparation for the advance, while attacks on targets immediately facing the troops were made on request from the battalion in the field.

During the advance to the Puriata, constant air attacks in the area immediately to the north of the river helped considerably to lower the morale of the enemy and break down his opposition. In support of the Australian's operations eastward from Mawaraka towards Mosigetta, Corsairs of No 20 Squadron were called on to clear an area of swamp and jungle immediately in front of the troops. Starting from a line only 80 yards in front of the foremost Australian position, the Corsairs combed the area thoroughly with 1,000 and 500lb stick bombs, depth charges, and by strafing.

A very successful close air support operation was carried out on 26 April, by forty-one Corsairs of Nos 14, 22 and 26 Squadrons. The target was a 700-yard section of road in the Hiru Hiru area, down which the Australian advance was blocked by strong Japanese defensive positions. In order to clear it, bombs had to be dropped in the jungle on either side of the road, 25 yards apart and 25 yards from the edge of the road, from a point 300 yards ahead of the most forward Australian troops. When the three fighter squadrons arrived over the target, it was marked by mortar bombs, and reconnaissance aircraft had laid smoke bombs along the line of the trail itself.

No 14 Squadron, led by Squadron Leader P. R. McNab, went in first with 1,000lb stick bombs and 325lb depth charges. The first section of four aircraft dropped their bombs on the left side of the road, and the next section bombed the right. The third and fourth sections treated the next hundred yards in the same manner. As soon as No 14 Squadron had finished their job, No 26 Squadron, led by Squadron Leader G. A. Delves, followed. After dropping their 1,000lb bombs, the Corsairs joined up in pairs and made strafing runs over the target. When they were clear, Squadron Leader J. R. Court led in No 22 Squadron, dropped 1,000lb bombs on the last section of road, and then strafed it thoroughly.

Air operations in northern Bougainville followed the same pattern as those in the south, softening-up raids behind enemy lines, and direct attacks on his forward positions when they were called for.

Strategic bombing on Bougainville in 1945 was directed mainly at Muguai in southern Bougainville, where Japanese 17th Army Headquarters was located. Up to April, most of the attacks on the area were launched from Piva, but in that month, RNZAF Corsairs and Venturas, and US Army Mitchells operating from

Top left: A formation of No 18 Squadron RNZAF Corsairs flying off the coast of Guadalcanal, 1945./*IWM*

Centre left: A RNZAF F4U-1D flying over the Ardmore Air Base in New Zealand./*IWM*

Bottom left: An RNZAF Corsair attached to No 5 Servicing Unit./*Jim Sullivan*

Above: A RNZAF F4U-1 of the No 4 Operational Training Unit during a training mission from the Ardmore Air Base, 1944./*John Regan*

Green Island were responsible for these attacks. In addition to scheduled strikes, a number of others were made when bad weather to the north prevented operations from Green Island against Rabaul and New Ireland.

In the early part of 1945, many bombing strikes were made by RNZAF Corsairs on barges, camps, and other targets in the Rabaul area. Operations over the Gazelle Peninsula from March on were confined mainly to security patrols. Whenever the weather permitted, flights of four Corsairs flew dawn to dusk patrols, denying the Japanese the use of their airfields. Enemy opposition was limited to anti-aircraft fire, which varied in intensity and accuracy; the weather was usually a more formidable hazard.

Nos 14 and 16 Squadrons had a disastrous day on 15 January 1945. Twelve Corsairs from Green Island and twenty from Piva had made a combined bombing attack on Toboi, a few miles southwest of Rabaul. Immediately after the attack, Flight Lieutenant F. G. Keefe of No 14 Squadron, was hit by anti-aircraft fire, he baled out and landed in Simpson Harbour.

Keefe was an exceptionally fine swimmer, and he headed out to sea. In the middle of the afternoon, after he had been swimming for six hours, the tide and wind changed direction, and he began to drift back into the harbour. All through the day he was covered by aircraft of Nos 14 and 16 Squadrons. A Catalina rescue aircraft stood by, but anti-aircraft fire prevented it from going in to rescue him. Two rafts were dropped, one falling within 300 yards of him, but he was not seen attempting to use them.

At sundown, with their fuel running low, the patrolling Corsairs were forced to leave and return to Green Island. On the way back, they ran into a tropical storm. Flying in darkness through torrential rain, five of the Corsairs crashed into the sea. One crashed at Green Island as it was about to land, and a seventh simply disappeared. An intensive search the next morning failed to find any trace of the missing pilots or their aircraft.

After the war it was reported by Japanese who were captured at Rabaul that Keefe had swum ashore, and later had taken a small boat and tried to row out of the harbour. A wounded arm made it impossible for him to row properly and he was taken prisoner by a Japanese naval party. He died of his wounds while a prisoner of war.

In addition to regular patrols over

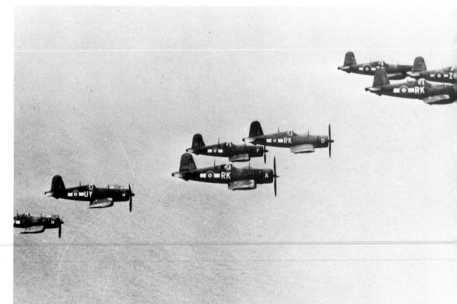

Rabaul, Green Island-based RNZAF Corsairs took part in a number of bombing strikes in April and the early part of May on Japanese bases in southern Bougainville, releasing the Piva-based squadrons for an all-out effort in support of the Australian ground forces. Attacks were also made on targets on Buka and northern Bougainville.

The RNZAF maintained fighter squadrons at Emirau until August 1945, when all forces were withdrawn from the island. The fighter squadrons operating there were Nos 14, 19, 22, 23, and 25. Operations there followed much the same pattern as they had since the RNZAF was first established on the island. Fighter activities were directed at keeping a constant patrol over Kavieng during daylight and dropping occasional bombs to harass the enemy. In addition, formations of up to eight fighter aircraft took part in strikes on designated targets, when they were required.

In February, and again in May, June, and July, RNZAF Venturas and US Army Mitchells from Emirau Island joined with RNZAF Corsairs from Green Island in a number of combined attacks on Rabaul.

In June 1945, all RNZAF units on Emirau Island were ordered to prepare to move forward, with Borneo their ultimate destination.

RNZAF forces on Los Negros during 1945 consisted of one Servicing Unit; a Corsair Assembly Unit, which was transferred from Espiritu Santo in February; and a succession of fighter squadrons: Nos 14, 17, 19, and 25. Fighter operations consisted of dawn and dusk patrols and scrambles to intercept

unidentified aircraft. When interceptions were made, the strangers invariably turned out to be friendly, but there were occasions when the aircraft evaded interception and were presumed to be Japanese.

Australian forces occupied Jacquinot Bay on the southeast coast of New Britain in November 1944. RNZAF units were established there in May 1945, and even though a few fighters were available for scramble alert duty in mid-May, the RNZAF units were not ready to undertake regular operations until the end of the month. At the end of May, No 20 Squadron began to carry out offensive patrols over the Rabaul area, strafing Japanese troops and barges, and bombing targets of opportunity. Weather permitting, five patrols were flown daily through the middle of July. After that, until the squadron ceased operations near the end of the war, their missions consisted mainly of concentrated bombing attacks on selected targets by formations of up to twelve Corsair aircraft.

When the Japanese finally surrendered on 2 September 1945, all RNZAF fighter squadrons, with the exception of those on leave and reforming in New Zealand, were operating in the Solomons-Bismarcks area. Four were on Bougainville, two at Los Negros, and three at Jacquinot Bay. A final move forward to Borneo had been planned, but had not yet taken place.

No 14 Squadron saw service in Japan after the war as part of the Occupation Forces from March 1946, to November 1948. By May 1949, all RNZAF Corsairs had been decommissioned.

Top left: An RNZAF F4U-1D taking off with a load of three drop tanks (centre-line 178 gallon tank; 150-gallon tanks on twin wing centre section pylons). /*d'E. C. Darby*

Centre left, above: RNZAF Corsairs taxiing out for a mission at an unknown South Pacific location./*d'E. C. Darby*

Centre left, below: RNZAF Corsairs of No 4 Servicing Unit parked at Mokerang, in the Admiralty Islands./*d'E. C. Darby*

Bottom left: A formation of RNZAF Corsairs of No 3 (RK), No 5 (ZG) and No 26 (UY) Serving Units from Ardmore Air Base./*d'E. C. Darby*

Below: An RNZAF FG-1D of No 14 Squadron in post-war markings at Haneda Airport, Japan, 27 November 1946. No 14 Squadron served in Japan as part of the Occupation Forces from March 1946, to November 1948./*Jim Sullivan*

The New -4

Vought Aircraft began initial engineering work on a new Corsair, the F4U-4, in May 1943. The first production F4U-4 made its maiden flight on 20 September 1944. Navy enthusiasm for the new fighter, particularly on the basis of the F4U-1's combat record in the South Pacific, resulted in the award of contracts for a total of 6,049 F4U-4s. It was this version that was in production at the rate of approximately 300 airplanes per month at the time of the Japanese surrender.

Equipped with the new Pratt and Whitney R-2800-18W 'C' series engine and a four-bladed 13ft 2in diameter Hamilton-Standard propeller, the new Corsair was rated as a 450mph fighter. The F4U-4 had a sea level rate of climb of 4,000 feet per minute, and a service ceiling of 41,600 feet. This new Corsair was to be the Navy's answer to the much-improved Japanese fighters starting to appear in the Pacific.

The -18W engine featured lengthened connecting rods and cylinder barrels that resulted in a power increase to 2,070hp at 2,800rpm at sea level, and 1,800hp at 29,300 feet at the military rating. The normal rating provided 1,640hp at 2,600rpm at 29,900 feet. The war emergency power rating (with water injection) was 2,450hp at 2,800rpm at sea level.

The greater power of the new 'C' series engine resulted in the need for larger oil coolers and intercoolers, and for more carburettor air. The result was the addition of an auxiliary stage air intake in the bottom part of the engine cowl. This intake crowded out the exhaust stacks previously located at the bottom of the cowl, and these were re-routed to two outlets above the wing and one below.

The F4U-4's normal gross weight was 12,500lbs, and it was armed with six 50-calibre machine guns. Later, the cannon-armed F4U-4B version went into production, with four 20-millimetre M-3 automatic cannons in place of the machine guns. The F4U-4 and -4B had provisions to carry eight five-inch wing-mounted rockets, and could also carry either two 150-gallon drop tanks, two 1,000lb bombs, or two 11.75-in rockets on twin pylons located beneath the wing centre section.

By the end of 1944, Vought was producing 300 Corsairs a month, or one complete airplane every 82 minutes. A total of 5,380 Corsairs was built during the year; Vought built 2,673; Brewster, 599; and Goodyear, 2,108.

Below: The prototype F4U-4 Corsair, the F4U-4X, which was an F4U-1 Flying Test Bed fitted with the F4U-4's Pratt & Whitney R-2800-18W 'C' series powerplant installation. */US National Archives*

Top left: An F4U-4 carrying a load of 5-inch high velocity aerial rockets (HVAR).
/*Vought Aircraft via Art Schoeni*

Centre left: The first USMC squadrons to receive the new F4U-4s were VMF-212 and VMF-223 on Okinawa, 15 May 1945./*US National Archives*

Below: The first production Vought F4U-4 Corsair, an XF4U-4, at the Naval Air Test Center, Patuxent River, Maryland, 24 March 1945. /*US National Archives*

Below: An F4U-1D of USMC
Squadron VMF-124 or VMF-213
aboard the USS *Essex* (CVE-9),
1 January 1945.
/US National Archives

Onto the Carriers

The Corsairs ended 1944 by going aboard the fast carriers with both US Navy and Marine pilots assigned to fly them. Assignment to shipboard duty was the year's supreme accomplishment for the Corsairs. And it came none too soon, as the Japanese were threatening the entire US Fleet with Kamikaze attacks, and their new fighters were also getting better and faster. As a result of the growing Kamikaze threat, VMF-124, the first Marine squadron to take Corsairs into combat, also became the first to operate from a carrier.

The Pacific Fleet high command, in a conference at Pearl Harbour, on 24-26 November 1944, expressed much alarm at the kamikaze threat. A decision was made to increase the number of fighters aboard the carriers. To accomplish this, the Navy called on the Marines and their Corsairs. The result was that on 28 December 1944, VMF-124, with Lieutenant Colonel William A. Millington commanding, and VMF-213, with Major David E. Marshall commanding, went aboard the fast carrier USS *Essex*. Boarding the ship in Ulithi Harbour, the two squadrons operated as one under the command of Millington. Prior to going aboard the *Essex*, the pilots of both squadrons had qualified for carrier landings aboard the USS *Saratoga*, USS *Makassar Strait,* and USS *Battan.* They were destined to make their first strike against Okinawa on 3 January 1945.

Air Operations Memorandum No. 70
9 March 1945
The F4U Gets in the Carrier War
From January reports covering the activity of VMF-124 and VMF-213, while part of Air Group Four, come the first accounts of the performance of the Corsair and its pilots in carrier combat operations. In summary conclusion to his operations report for the two Marine squadrons, Lieutenant Colonel Millington, acting Air Group Commander, said:

"The Corsair fighter could well be adapted to aircraft carrier use if it were limited to purposes for which it was designed; namely, fighter missions, as such. If it could be utilised for interceptions, bomber escorts, strafing, and rocket attacks only, its performance would show up to a much higher degree. To accomplish this best performance, a streamlined centreline belly tank must be incorporated and a streamlined rocket-rack installation made, accommodating from four to six five-inch head, five-inch motor rockets. (Present eight-place rocket racks are too bulky and air resistant.) Removal of pylons is advisable, as they would then serve no purpose. Rocket attacks have proved to be far more accurate and effective on strikes and sweeps than bombing attacks. The fault may well lie in pilot training largely, but also in the fighter's characteristics; however, the fact remains

that fighters are far more effective with rockets than with bombs.

"The Corsair's performance in takeoffs and landings is good once the pilot becomes familiar with the plane in various loading conditions. Hence, it is recommended that all pilots qualify aboard carriers with the airplane in those various conditions before coming out to the fleet. The airplane itself must be improved in regard to its wing-folding characteristics to expedite handling on the deck.

"The Corsair as its stands now does not possess the all-around carrier characteristics of the Grumman Hellcat, but as the war progresses, it may well be that there will be a growing need for a fighter interceptor squadron for each carrier, and, as such, the Corsair would serve well."

From the Ship's Point of View-
The ship's report stated, with respect to performance of the Corsairs:

"Numerous operating difficulties presented themselves which unfortunately had to be solved during

combat and in consistently foul weather. Under the circumstances, comparatively high operational losses were inevitable. However, prior to the close of the period, considerable progress was made. Squadron commanders and senior officers of the ship are in accord as to the nature of the difficulties involved and their solution."

Some of the more important details from the ship's viewpoint were then set forth in the report, excerpts from which are as follows:

Personnel — "Confronted with the difficult assignment of going into combat as carrier-based squadrons without benefit of a shakedown cruise to accustom them to carrier operations, the Marine squadrons performed most creditably. Their discipline, cooperation, and eagerness to increase their effectiveness were very commendable and made them welcome aboard ship."

Training — "The pilots had had an average of approximately 400 hours flight time in Corsairs, but an average of only about 12 carrier landings. All carrier

qualifications had been flown in Corsairs in full light condition; i.e., without ammunition, bombs, or auxiliary tank. One of the greatest single causes of plane and pilot loss during this operating period was weather and the relative inexperience of the Marine pilots in instrument flying. Eight F4Us were lost at sea, practically all under instrument flying conditions. (F6Fs flying under the same conditions at the same time all returned aboard.) The lack of an adequate instrument training syllabus increased materially the hazard confronting pilots called upon to perform missions under weather conditions considered difficult even by experienced instrument pilots."

Flight Characteristics and Limitations
General — "The F4U, with greater speed, rate of climb and manoeuvrability than the F6F, is superior as an intercept fighter. However, at the present stage, it lacks the versatility of the F6F and is decidedly inferior as a fighter-bomber."
Stalling — "The F4U stalls easily at low speeds without any advance warning, such as the shuddering felt in an F6F, and tends to fall off on either wing. For this reason, two planes were lost just after

Top left: A VMF-124 or 213 F4U-1D about to land on the USS *Essex* (CVE-9), 1 January 1945. /US National Archives

Bottom left: An F4U-1D of VMF-124 or 213 landing aboard the USS *Essex* (CVE-9), 1 January 1945. /US National Archives

Above: An F4U-1D of VMF-124 or 213 preparing to takeoff from the USS *Essex* for a mission against Formosa. /US National Archives

takeoff, and another while making its final turn to come aboard.

Auxiliary Tanks — "Both the centreline and pylon tanks begin to buffet at speeds in excess of 250 knots, thus preventing a dive with tank attached. There is considerable difficulty in releasing the tanks, especially in the case of the centreline.

Flight Deck Prodedure

Launching — "Because of the lack of experience of the Marine pilots in carrier operations in the F4U-1D with ammunition and auxiliary tank, a considerable safety factor was added to available performance figures in determining the amount of deck run required. It was determined that for initial operations the minimum deck run should be 500 feet with 30 knots over the deck and 450 feet with 33 knots. Whenever additional deck was available over this minimum, up to 50 additional feet would be allowed during launches early in the period. Despite this margin of safety, two planes crashed on takeoff during the first two days of operations, both in spins. However, as pilot technique improved, the amount of deck run was decreased until at the end of the period, the normal spot was the same as that employed for the F6F under similar

loadings — a minimum of 450 feet with 30 knots, a minimum of 550 feet with 30 knots for an added weight of 500lbs of bombs.

Catapulting — "Of the two types of auxiliary tanks fitted to the F4U-1D, the diameter and location of the centreline tank and the location of the catapult hooks are such that the catapult bridle will not clear the sides of the tank. Accordingly, the pylon tank was tried first so as to permit catapulting. However, the pilots complained of a yawing effect, which was believed due to the off-centre location of the pylon tank. Thus, it was necessary to resort to the centreline tank and forego catapulting, despite the reduced efficiency of operations. When the centreline tanks were exhausted, the use of pylon tanks was resumed and the pilots, being then more experienced, accommodated themselves to this tank without further difficulty. The Corsair was frequently catapulted with a single pylon tank installed.

Recoveries — "Except for its tendency to stall, the carrier landing characteristics of the F4U are quite satisfactory. However, the following should be avoided: (a) a long approach in the groove is bad from the standpoint of poor pilot visibility; (b) a high and slow approach is apt to result in a buckled fuselage or a failure of the tailwheel yoke assembly; and (c) too fast an approach will cause the Corsair to bounce along the deck.

"Normally, full flaps were used for landings. In this condition, the Corsair decelerates more rapidly than the Hellcat and can also accelerate more quickly. A low approach at a speed slightly less than that customarily used for the Hellcat was found to be preferable to the high and slow type of approach. During emergencies, Corsairs without flaps were successfully recovered. Only slightly greater speed was used than in a normal landing.

"Frequently, landing operations were conducted in rough to heavy seas. Then particularly was the apparent weakness of the tail wheel yoke assembly noticeable. Operational figures support the view that barrier crashes resulted more from the limited carrier experience of Corsair pilots than for other reasons. During the first two weeks of the operations, five Corsairs caught barriers, while three barrier crashes occurred during the remainder of the period, only one of which took place during the last nine operating days.

Deck Handling — "Tow bars and pins, both tail and nose, used with the F6F

Top left: Cannon-armed VMF-311 'Helles Belles' F4U-1C Corsairs aboard the USS *Breton* (CVE-23). The first time these guns were fired in combat was 7 April 1945, when five VMF-311 pilots shot down a Lily that was making a kamikaze charge toward the carrier USS *Sitkoh Bay* off the island of Okinawa. */US National Archives*

Bottom left: An F4U-1D of VMF-124 or 213 preparing to takeoff from the USS *Essex* (CVE-9), 1 January 1945. */US National Archives*

Above: VMF-124 or 213 F4U-1Ds aboard the USS *Essex* (CVE-9) prior to a raid in the Tokyo area, 27 February 1945. */US National Archives*

123

served equally well in spotting the F4U. However, operations are slowed, both during launches and recoveries, largely because of the F4U's hydraulic wing-folding mechanism which functions slowly. It was found helpful during spreading of wings to cock the plane at alternate angles to the wind as it was being brought up the deck, so as to use the wind force to start the spreading of the wings. Both folding and spreading is accomplished more rapidly with low, rather than high, engine rpm. Another help in speeding up launches and recoveries is the station of two mechanics so that they are constantly available to help pilots with wing spreading or folding.

From the Squadron's Operations Report —
The following points excerpted from the operations report of the two squadrons will supplement the foregoing from the ship's report. Regarding landings and takeoffs, the report notes that "after a week of operations, all pilots became more confident in handling the airplane. A full realisation of the necessity of precision flying, particularly in takeoff procedures, has seemed to reduce our troubles."

Instrument Flying —
"The pilot's have learned a bitter lesson in the importance of knowing their instruments and relying on them. In this past operation, we sustained an operational loss of seven pilots, five of them being attributed directly to becoming lost in bad weather, and the pilots did a remarkably good job in carrying out their missions. But losses would have been lowered considerably if adequate basic instrument training had been followed vigorously. Too many pilots treat instrument training lightly only to suffer in the extreme for it under combat conditions."

Further stressed in the report are radio procedure and reports, recognition, navigation, and similar basic elements of successful carrier operation which have received repeated and deserved emphasis in the Air Operations Memorandum.

Air Operations Memorandum No. 70 9 March 1945
F4Us in Action
Encounters by the Marine Corsairs of VMF-124 and VMF-213 with enemy aircraft in the month's operations were infrequent, but when enemy planes were sighted, the Marines made them very unhappy. Their best day came on 20 January, when, in the neighbourhood of

Formosa, 12 F4Us in three flights were flying CAP over the force. This was along toward dark when the enemy likes to bare his teeth. At about 1700, a four-plane division led by Captain Kersey was vectored into a bogey which turned out to be four twin-engined bombers, later identified as Helens, flying at 12,000 feet. The Corsairs came in from above and out of the sun, achieving complete surprise on their first run. Kersey and his wingman, Second Lieutenant Batson, made three overhead runs on one Helen just over a DD (destroyer) picket which reported it splashed. They immediately picked up another Helen below the cloud base of 220 feet, chased it towards the DD picket, and had to pull up into the cloud at full gun to escape AA from the DD.

Meanwhile, Lieutenants Boutte and Stallings were after one of the other four Helens. Stallings, swishing 15 degrees to either side of the Helen's tail, riddled the fuselage from tail to cockpit, as well as both wings, with several long bursts. The bomber which had been making steadily for cloud cover, fell off suddenly in a straight-down dive. Following into the overcast, Boutte saw it crash in the sea. The pilot had apparently been killed.

Another division headed by Lieutenant McGill had been vectored on another bogey at about the same time. This too was found to be a covey of four Helens, also at 12,000 feet. McGill, in a high side attack on one of them, was sucked flat and fired until forced to push over or collide. The Helen was firing 20mm from

the tail turret, and as McGill closed, began throwing what appeared to be tin cans about one-foot square from the tail, port side. The Jap started smoking in the starboard engine and went into a port side spiral from which he never recovered. Another Helen following the smoking plane to port attracted McGill's attention and he made three high side runs, sucking flat after each one, and firing until nearly coming into the bomber. This Helen was also firing from its tail and throwing off the can-like objects. (No explosion was noted but McGill was flying very close to the planes.) Going into the clouds with this Helen, McGill broke out at 1,500 feet in time to see it and the first Helen splash in the sea about one-half mile and fifteen seconds apart. Lieutenant Strom also saw the double dip.

Working over still another Helen, Second Lieutenant Kehoe of this division, set its engine afire by hits from 15 deg above and slightly to port. This one exploded at about 500 feet.

About 1740, another vector was given this flight, and another Helen tallyhoed about 30 miles from base. Strom and Barberi made overhead runs and believed they got hits. McGill and Kehoe then latched on to it, and McGill again performed the 'high side sucked flat' manoeuvre, firing until forced to pull up to avoid collision. This again did the trick, burning the Helen at the right wing root, and she plummetted into the sea.

The third division of the CAP got its first vector about 1740, went out and

Top left: F4U-1D's of VMF-216 or 217 on board the USS *Wasp* (CVE-18) prior to a raid in the Tokyo area, 16 February 1945. */US National Archives*

Bottom left: A USN F4U-1D of Navy Fighter Squadron VF-84 about to be launched from the USS *Bunker Hill* (CVE-17) for a strike in the Tokyo Area, 16 February 1945. */US National Archives*

Below: Yellow-nosed VF-84 F4U-1D Corsairs on board the USS *Bunker Hill* (CVE-17). */Pratt & Whitney Aircraft*

found a Sally about 30 miles from base. Lieutenant Knight saw this one first, edged over early in a flat side run, firing within range in a three-second burst. His bullets struck the Sally in the port engine and cockpit, possibly killing the pilot. She fell, hit the water, and sank, though not burning.

Ten minutes later, Captain Bedford and Second Lieutenant Boyd of this division spotted another Sally at 10 o'clock and on their same level, 2,000 feet. Dropping their belly tanks and applying full power, they closed rapidly. Bedford, firing on a beam run, 30 deg deflection, recovered above the Sally and slowed to 160 knots to stay behind. Boyd was firing at this time, and as he slid out, Bedford closed, no deflection, firing for at least 20 seconds. That did it. Pictures were taken of the Sally burning in the water.

The CAP secured at 1820, having destroyed eight twin-engine bombers; six thought to be Helens, and two Sallys.

Left: A USN F4U-1D Corsair belonging to the Navy's 'Grim Reapers' Fighter Squadron, VF-10, from the USS *Intrepid* (CVE-11) near Okinawa, 10 April 1945.
/US National Archives

Below: An F4U-4 from the USS *Lake Champlain* (CVE-39).
/US National Archives

Bottom: USMC VMF-311 F4U-1Cs and VMF-441 F4U-1Ds aboard the USS *Breton* (CVE-23), 7 April 1945. These Corsairs were being catapulted from the carrier for the first landings on Yonton Airfield, Okinawa.
/US National Archives

The Final Year

After spending most of 1944 in clean-up actions in the South and Central Pacific, the Corsairs were now with Task Force 38 and were destined to become the finest naval fighters of World War II.

The final year of the war, 1945, was to see shipboard Corsairs venture into the China Sea, fight at Iwo Jima, Okinawa, in the Tokyo Raids, and over the Philippines and Formosa. Carrier-based Corsairs, flown by the US Navy and Marine Corps, opened the new year 3 January 1945, with a slashing attack on Okinawa. Then, they moved on with Task Force 38 to the South China Sea to take part in the 'Navy's greatest day of the war', the 12 January raid on Saigon — the first attacks on the Asian mainland by the US Navy since the start of the war. Operating both as fighters and fighter-

bombers, the F4Us claimed at least a portion of the raid's final tally of enemy ships sunk; 14 warships and 33 merchant vessels.

Corsairs next hit Tokyo in the diversionary raids flown in preparation to the invasion of Iwo Jima. Bad weather, however, reduced the effectiveness of the raids. Corsair pilots of VMF-112, who were operating from the USS *Bennington*, shot down a Betty on the way into Tokyo, shot down a twin-engined Nick, and destroyed 20 planes on the ground. *Essex*-based Corsairs flew fighter sweeps in the Tokyo area, claiming four shootdowns, 12 destroyed and five probably destroyed on the ground at Tenryu Airfield on 16 February. Rocket-carrying Corsairs also went into action, hitting 15 parked planes at Haramachide Airfield on February 17.

Below: USMC FG-1Ds and F4U-1Cs on Iwo Jima en route to Okinawa, 18 April 1945. */USMC via Rowland Gill*

Corsairs based aboard four *Essex*-class carriers supported the Iwo Jima landings of the US Marine Corps. As the troops hit the beach, a flight of 24 Corsairs led by Millington dropped napalm, fired rockets, and strafed just 200 yards ahead of the leathernecks. Prior to this low-level attack, Millington was reportedly told by Colonel Vernon Megee, the landing force commander, to 'go in and scrape your bellies on the beach'. Corsairs from the USS *Wasp* and USS *Hornet* elicited a 'well done' for their part in the glide-bombing activities during the landings.

Following the Iwo Jima landings, Corsairs with the newly formed Task Force 58 moved on to help soften up the Japanese homeland island of Kyushu in preparation for the invasion of Okinawa. On 23 March 1945, Corsairs from VMF-112 and VMF-123, together with VF-82, destroyed 26 suicide boats and damaged military installations in the Okinawa area. On 3 April, a dozen Corsairs, flown by Marines from the USS *Bunker Hill*, teamed up with 16 Navy Hellcats to attack Amami O Shima and Kikai Jima. They ran into a large number of Zekes, who attempted to ram the Corsairs. The Marines shot down 11, and the Navy pilots got the rest. Air activity for the carrier-based Corsairs increased heavily with the pending invasion of Okinawa.

Above: USMC F4U-1Cs on the muddy Yonton Airfield, Okinawa, April 1945.
/USMC via Rowland Gill

Left: VMF-312 FG-1D Corsairs, which were operating from Okinawa's Kadena Airfield, April 1945./*USMC via Rowland Gill*

Above: A USMC F4U-1D carrying a load of two Napalm tanks and 5-inch rockets over Okinawa during the final stages of World War II.

/US Navy via Harold Andrews

Air Operations Memorandum No 82 25 May 1945

VMF-123 meets Jap First Team

Although there have been many reports of the deteriorating quality of Jap pilots in recent months, VMF-123 can testify that the enemy fliers they mixed with near Kure on 19 March were anything but scrub league. The 15 Corsairs in the action were launched from the USS *Bennington* before dawn and were jumped from the rear by about 30 Japs just after crossing the Honshu coast. One division of F4Us turned to meet the attackers, and its leader Captain DeFabio, saw Zekes coming in two sections. The enemy planes bracketed the Corsairs and then drove from left to right in sections. Their formations were excellent and their tactics ably performed. The planes from the right hit the Corsairs on their left, and vice versa.

Japs Use US Tactics —

Major Thomas E. Mobley, Jr, the squadron commander, was impressed by the marked similarity between the Japanese tactics in this engagement and the usual American air tactics. He notes that all attacks were well coordinated and nearly always by two-plane sections. "The Japs struck at our planes when the F4Us were on the outside of their turns, and enemy marksmanship and airmanship were as fine as the squadron has ever seen, with tracers on our planes

as soon as the Japs opened fire and no wandering all over the sky trying to get the angle of fire." Mobley also notes that some of the enemy planes came in for straight attacks on the Corsair's tails and then broke away when fired upon in a split-S. They also used the scissors attack to good advantage, hitting at opposite sides of our formations.

Despite the numerical advantage of the Japs and their much better than average skill, the Marines dished out considerably more punishment than they took. Two Corsairs were hit and went down on the enemy's first pass, but in the following few minutes, six Japs were destroyed, and as the battle continued, three more were accounted for with no further losses of Marine pilots, although a number of the Corsairs were heavily damaged. Mobley comments: "The F4U-1D is still a mighty hard plane to knock down. The planes that came back were in most instances exceedingly sad-looking, but they were still flying."

Okinawa was invaded on 1 April 1945, with Corsairs playing a supporting role. The Corsairs were kept so busy with kamikazes during the first few weeks of the operation that close air support was a secondary consideration. However, as the kamikaze threat diminished, Corsairs were able to support ground troops with increasing quantities of rockets, bombs, and napalm. Land-based Marines flew 600 support missions between 7-30 April.

In one action with the kamikazes, the Corsairs of VMF-411 shot down 17 planes. One Corsair pilot was so hot on the tail of a kamikaze that he knocked one of the radar antennas off the destroyer USS *Laffey* during the chase. The kamikaze also knocked off one of the Laffey's yardarms. Both planes crashed into the water, and the Corsair pilot was rescued.

On 18 April, Corsairs treated the Japanese to the first napalm they had dropped. Between that date and the final securing of Okinawa, Marines alone were to spew 152,000 gallons of the liquid fire across the island.

Three lost Marines added a note of comedy to carrier operations off Okinawa on 1 May. At 30,000 feet on patrol in their Corsairs over northern Okinawa, the three Marines wandered several hundred miles out to sea. They were almost out of fuel when the carrier USS *Yorktown* picked up their distress calls and directed them to land on board. None of the Marines had ever made a carrier landing. One of them, after setting his Corsair down perfectly, was reported to have asked:

"What was that man doing waving those paddles back there?"

"Brother," he was told, "he's the landing signal officer and he was giving you a wave-off!"

First Lieutenant Robert Klingman, another Corsair pilot, chased after a fast Nick two-seater fighter that was on a photographic reconnaissance mission at 38,000 feet. When his guns froze in the severe cold, he knocked the airplane down by ramming it with the Corsair's big propeller. His Corsair, missing part of its propeller, and with part of the Jap's shorn-off tail imbedded in its cowling, brought Klingman back to Okinawa.

In his first aerial combat, Second Lieutenant William Eldridge, Jr, shot down four Japanese planes in four minutes. The planes, all suicide bombers, were shot down less than 300 miles from the Japanese mainland.

Instances like those were just a few of hundreds that led Marine fighter pilots to dub their Corsairs the 'Sweethearts of Okinawa'. VMF-323 pilots shot down 124.5 Japanese planes in a whirlwind tour of duty on Okinawa without losing one of their own. Major George Axtell, who took VMF-323 into action, was reported to have said of the Corsair: "It's the best fighter there is. It's rugged. It's a workhorse. You can use it for anything, including dive-bombing, and it's effective. You can shoot anything off or out of that plane and still it goes". F4U-4s had started arriving on Okinawa by the end of May, and by the end of the Okinawa campaign nearly every carrier the Navy had was equipped with Corsairs.

Air Operations Memorandum No 94
24 August 1945
Outnumbered Corsairs Down 6, Lose 2
Battling against overwhelming odds and skilled and aggressive pilots, Marine Corsairs of VMF-113, based at Ie Shima, shot down six enemy aircraft and probably destroyed three others off Amami O Shima on 22 June. Two Corsairs were lost and three others damaged heavily.

Of the 18 Corsairs sent aloft to form a barrier CAP, only the eight stationed 'high' at 15,000 feet participated in the battle against an estimated 44 Japs, flying Zekes, Franks, and Georges. The Nips used their familiar deception tactics at the outset, sending in one division of four planes 'low' at 17,000 feet as decoys. As the Corsairs rose to attack, two large enemy groups appeared. Each contained at least five four-plane divisions. With a 5,000-foot altitude advantage, one group headed for the Corsairs from 12 o'clock and the other from 6 o'clock.

In the wild melee that followed, one Marine Second Lieutenant shot down two Zekes, and damaged a third before he, in turn, apparently was shot down. The other mission pilot also splashed a Zeke before radioing: "I am all shot to hell and heading back to base." First Lieutenant J. D. Johnson and Second Lieutenants C. H. Jones and A. C. Frazer downed a Zeke, George, and Frank, respectively, while Johnson and First Lieutenant R. Huncher scored 'probables.' The Corsairs of Johnson, Frazer, and Huncher were damaged.

"The enemy planes and pilots engaged were by no means of the type usually encountered," the squadron report said. "Their planes were good and the pilots skilled and aggressive. A very good formation was flown and maintained. Deception was used by sending in one division as a decoy. The planes waiting above were grouped in four-plane divisions, sections roughly abreast, and divisions stacked.

"They attacked by division in the following manner: the whole division executed a chandelle to the left, thus starting a diving approach on opposite course with altitude advantage. The division then split into two sections, one

Above: In June 1945, USMC Lieutenant David D. Duncan crawled into a modified auxiliary fuel tank that was slung under the port wing of a US Army F-5E Lightning of the 28th Photo Recon Squadron and took off to photograph USMC Corsairs striking Japanese positions in the mountains of Southern Okinawa. Here, the F-5E and at least two four-plane divisions of F4Us near the target, the Kushi-Take stronghold on Okinawa. The Corsairs are armed with two Napalm tanks on their twin wing centre section pylons and 5-inch rockets./*USMC via Rowland Gill*

Top: The F-5E followed the Corsairs in on their target runs, and Lieutenant Duncan photographed this Corsair just as the pilot was firing a rocket broadside towards an enemy position.
/*US National Archives*

going to each side of the target planes and executed high side runs simultaneously, completing the run by tailing in and joining up.''

Air Operations Memorandum No 93 17 August 1945
Marines Find F4U-4 Superior to Tojo
In their first combat test of F4U-4s, four VMF-223 fighter pilots each shot down a Tojo on 21 June while on Barrier Combat Air Patrol between Yokoate and Kikai in the Nansei Shoto. Lack of aggressiveness on the part of the Nips, who outnumbered the Corsairs three to one, prevented any detailed comparison of the combat performance of the two types of aircraft. Pilots said, however, that the new Corsairs could definitely out-climb, out-dive, and out-fly the Jap army fighter. Lieutenants M. T. Tiernan, J. C. Groot, A. C. Evans, and R. A. McAlister each got credit for a kill.

Below: A USMC F4U-1D carring
a load of three drop tanks.
/US National Archives

Above: Marine Air Group 45 mechanics working on a VMF-114 'Death Dealers' Corsair in the engineering area on Falalop Island, 10 August 1945.
/US National Archives

In the final year of the war up to V-J Day, 3,387 Corsairs were produced, 1,932 by Vought, and 1,455 by Goodyear.

The Corsair's record with the US Marine Corps and Navy from Guadalcanal to V-J Day is impressive, as is shown in the following tabulation of the Corsair's World War II combat record.

Combat Record of the Corsair
with US Marine Corps and US Navy during World War II
(Based on combat operating statistics provided by the Navy Department)

Total enemy aircraft destroyed in air combat by Corsairs, land and carrier-based	2,140
Total Corsairs destroyed in air combat by enemy aircraft	189
Ratio of enemy aircraft shot down to Corsair losses	11.3 to 1
Total action sorties carried out by Corsairs	64,051
Targets of sorties:	
Enemy Airfields	10,210
Other Military Targets	32,770
Land Transportation	2,818
Harbour Areas	2,095
Other and Unknown Land Targets	11,656
Armoured Warships	263
Unarmoured Warships	245
Merchantmen (over 500 tons)	799
Merchantmen (under 500 tons)	3,172
Ships (Type Unknown)	23
Corsair losses (in addition to 189 destroyed in air combat)	
By enemy anti-aircraft	349
Operational during action sorties	230
On other flights	692
On ship or on ground	164

Above: A USMC ground crewman arming a 1000lb bomb which is mounted on a later model Brewster-type centre-line bomb rack on Falalop Island, 10 August 1945. */US National Archives*

Combat record comparison of Land-based and Carrier-based Corsairs with US Marine Corps and US Navy during World War II

	Land-based	Carrier-based
Enemy fighters destroyed in air combat by Marine Corsairs	1,100	159
Enemy bombers destroyed in air combat by Marine Corsairs	300	59
Total enemy aircraft destroyed in air combat by Marine Corsairs	1,400	218
Enemy fighters destroyed in air combat by Navy Corsairs	132	147
Enemy bombers destroyed in air combat by Navy Corsairs	4	237
Total enemy aircraft destroyed in air combat by Navy Corsairs	136	384
Enemy aircraft destroyed in air combat by Corsairs (Service not known)	2	
Total enemy aircraft destroyed in air combat by Marine and Navy Corsairs	1,538	602
Marine Corsairs destroyed in air combat by enemy aircraft	141	16
Marine Corsairs lost to enemy anti-aircraft	207	44
Marine Corsairs lost in operational accidents during action sorties	157	21
Total Marine Corsairs lost on action sorties	505	81
Navy Corsairs destroyed in air combat by enemy aircraft	14	18
Navy Corsairs lost to enemy anti-aircraft	5	93
Navy Corsairs lost in operational accidents during action sorties	4	48
Total Navy Corsairs lost on action sorties	23	159
Total Marine and Navy Corsairs lost on action sorties	528	240

Between the Wars

The US Navy, along with the Air Force, cancelled billions of dollars of aircraft procurement contracts following V-J Day, but the war-winning Corsair, which was doing full-time carrier duty with US Navy as well as Marine pilots, stayed in production. The F4U-4 contract was cut back to 2,356 airplanes and the production rate was reduced to 21 airplanes per month. The last of the 2,356 F4U-4s was delivered on 1 August 1947. Included in this number were 296 cannon-armed F4U-4Bs, one experimental F4U-4N night fighter, and nine F4U-4P photo reconnaissance versions.

Meanwhile, the most radically redesigned Corsair, the F4U-5, was under development at Vought. The XF4U-5 prototype made its first flight on 4 April 1946, and the first production version of

the F4U-5 flew on 12 May 1947. The F4U-5 was a high-altitude fighter, which was designed to operate at altitudes up to 45,000 feet. It was powered by a new R-2800-32W 'E' series Double Wasp engine with a two-stage, variable-speed supercharger, which developed approximately 200 horsepower more than the 'C' series engine used in the F4U-4.

The thrust line of the engine was drooped 2.75 degrees to improve the airplane's longitudinal stability characteristics and forward visibility, and twin cheek inlets were added at the 4 and 8 o'clock positions to provide air to the side-mounted superchargers. The canopy sides were bulged outward to improve rearward visibility. The outer wing panels, which had been fabric covered throughout the long life of the airplane,

were covered with metal, which resulted in a substantial drag reduction. A combustion heater was added in the lower fuselage behind the cockpit to provide both cabin heating and windshield defrosting. Pilot comfort was emphasised to a high degree with a completely modernised cockpit.

The maximum speed of the F4U-5 was 450mph at 32,000 feet. It had a sea level rate of climb of 4,500 feet per minute, and a service ceiling of 45,000 feet.

The basic armament of the F4U-5 consisted of four 20-millimetre M-3 automatic cannons. The F4U-5 had provisions to carry eight five-inch wing mounted rockets, and bombs weighing up to 1,600lbs, 11.75-inch rockets, or 150-gallon drop tanks could be carried on twin wing centre section pylons. One bomb, weighing up to 2,000lbs, could be carried on a centreline pylon. The normal gross weight of the F4U-5 was 12,900lbs.

Continuing interest in night and all-weather fighting led to the development of the F4U-5N night fighter Corsair. The F4U-5N could be easily distinguished from the F4U-5 day fighter by its radar nacelle, which was located far out on the starboard wing. The night fighter incorporated several features which were not installed in the F4U-5 day fighter. Some of these, in addition to the radar

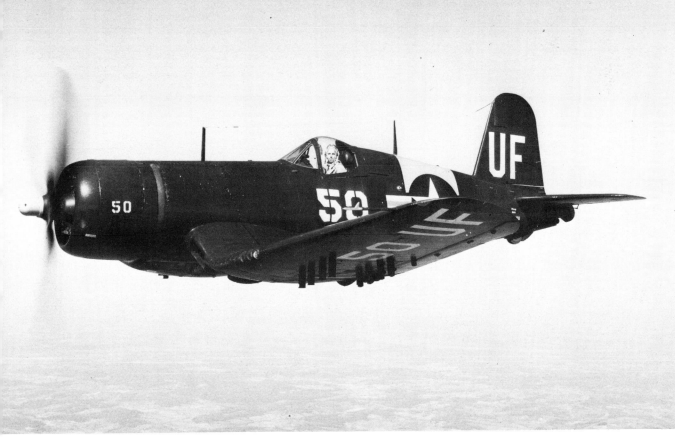

equipment, included VHF radio, gun muzzle flash hiders, and exhaust collector flame dampers.

The F4U-5N had the same load carrying capability as the F4U-5, but the radar nacelle installation reduced the maximum speed of the night fighter to approximately 435mph at 30,000 feet. Sea level rate of climb was reduced to 4,350 feet per minute, and the F4U-5N's service ceiling was 44,000 feet. The normal gross weight of the F4U-5N was 13,800lbs.

A further development of the F4U-5 day fighter was a photo reconnaissance version, the F4U-5P. Provisions were incorporated in the -5P for the installation of either a 'K' series aerial camera or a S-75 continuous strip camera. In order to accommodate the camera equipment, the remote compass transmitter had to be relocated in the vertical stabiliser. The F4U-5Ps were equipped with one vertical and two oblique sliding camera doors, an oil deflector for each of the doors, and special exhaust stack extensions. The F4U-5P's performance characteristics were essentially the same as the F4U-5, and it had the same armament carrying capability as the day fighter.

Far left, top: A formation of USN Fighter Squadron VF-14 F4U-4 Corsairs, 2 September 1949.
/US National Archives

Far left, bottom: A formation of USMC VMF-212 F4U-4 Corsairs, 1947.
/USMC via Harold Andrews

Left: F4U-5 Corsairs of USN Test Squadron VX-3, 26 July 1951.
/USN via Harold Andrews

Below: Marine Air Group 33 F4U-4 Corsairs at Marine Corps Air Station El Toro, California, 17 February 1948.
/USMC via Harold Andrews

Corsairs in Korea

Carrier-based Corsairs launched their first strikes of the Korean conflict on 3 July 1950, only eight days after the unexpected outbreak of hostilities on 25 June 1950. For two days, Corsairs and AD Skyraiders with the USS *Valley Forge*, together with Fireflies and Seafires from the HMS *Triumph,* attacked the communist airfields and railroad marshalling yards at Pyongyand and Onjong-Ni. Few of the airfield installations escaped damage, and most of the railroad yards, locomotives, and boxcars were destroyed during these successful raids.

The First Provisional Marine Brigade arrived in Pusan from the US on 2 August 1950. Two Marine fighter squadrons, VMF-214 and VMF-323, which were both

flying Corsairs, were immediately earmarked to provide close air support for the Marine infantry unit. During the first week in August, the Marine Corsairs embarked on the escort carriers USS *Sicily* and USS *Badoeng Strait.* During the days that followed, the Marine pilots flew an average of 45 attack missions per day, most of these in support of the first Marine Brigade. About this time, Marine night fighter squadron VMF(N)-513, which was equipped with F4U-5Ns, was attached to the 8th fighter-bomber wing at Itazuke in Japan. The squadron immediately began night intruder missions over Korea. Early in August, the VMF(N)-513 Corsairs joined USAF F-82 Twin Mustangs and B-26 Invaders on night interdiction missions. But, because

Below: A formation of USN F4U-4 Corsairs belonging to VF-783, from the USS *Bon Homme Richard* (CVE-31). /Jim Sullivan

Above: Naval Reserve Squadron
F4U-4s belonging to either
VF-884 or VF-791 flying past the
carrier to which they were
attached, the USS *Boxer* (CVE-
21) in Korean waters, 9 April
1951.
/US National Archives

Left: USN F4U-4 Corsairs
belonging to VF-63, from the USS
Boxer (CVE-21), 14 May 1952.
/US National Archives

Above: A Marine Attack Squadron VMA-312 'Checkerboard' F4U-4 Corsair about to be catapulted off the USS *Bairoko* (CVE-115) near Korea, 1 May 1952.
/US National Archives

Centre right: A VMF-312 'Checkerboard' F4U-4 landing aboard the USS *Bairoko* (CVE-115) on 11 February 1952, marking the first time during the Korean conflict that the squadron operated aboard a carrier.
/USMC via Rowland Gill

Below right: Maintenance being performed on VMF-312 'Checkerboard' Corsairs at Wonson Airfield, Korea, which the squadron shared with VMF(N)-513.
/USMC via Rowland Gill

Above: VMF(N)-513 'Flying Nightmares' F4U-5N night fighter Corsairs at Wonson Airfield, Korea, 2 November 1950./*USMC via Rowland Gill*

of their short range, their operations were restricted to attacks on enemy communication lines and artillery in the vicinity of the Pusan Perimeter. Nevertheless, the Corsairs accounted for up to ten of the 35 sorties flown per night by the Fifth Air Force's night intruders during August.

The landing at Inchon, which was far behind enemy lines, began on 15 September 1950. Air cover was provided throughout the operation by Navy Corsairs and Skyraiders from the USS *Valley Forge* and USS *Philippine Sea*, and Fireflies from the HMS *Triumph*. At dawn the following morning, Marines headed toward Kimpo Airfield near Seoul, the South Korean capital. The field was captured with little damage on 17 September. On 19 September, Corsairs of Marine Air Group 33, consisting of squadrons VMF(N)-542 and VMF-312, flew to Kimpo from the carriers USS *Sicily* and USS *Badoeng Strait*. Their place was taken by Marine Air Group 12, whose Corsairs were brought up from their transit base at Itami. The Kimpo-based Corsairs went into action almost immediately, covering the Marine crossing of the Han River on 20 September.

As North Korean resistance crumbled, Corsairs of Marine Air Group 33 flew over the shattered buildings of Seoul, dropping napalm on pockets of enemy resistance in the streets and surrounding hills. On the afternoon of 27 September, the city was captured.

The cold Korean winter prompted the development of a winterised version of the F4U-5N night fighter. This new night fighting Corsair was designated the F4U-5NL, and was equipped with wing and empennage de-icer boots, propeller blade de-icer shoes, and a windshield de-icing system. A total of 101 F4U-5NLs, were produced, along with 223 F4U-5 day fighters, 214 F4U-5Ns, and 30 F4U-5Ps. The last -5 version of the Corsair was delivered on 22 October 1951.

Marine Night Fighter Squadron VMF(N)-513 commenced an interdiction campaign against the main supply routes close to the front lines on 1 March 1951. These missions almost invariably teamed together C-47 flare-dropping aircraft and attacking F4Us and F7F Tigercats. Flying in relays from Pusan Airfield, the Marine night fighters met the C-47 flare-droppers over an assigned road, and both planes searched for enemy vehicles. When targets were located, the Marine pilot would request that the target be lighted with flares. After orienting himself in the flare light, the Marine fighter went down and attacked the target. After a fighter had strayed in the target area for about an hour and a half, it was usually relieved on station by a fresh fighter. During three months of operation, the crews of VMF(N)-513 estimated that they had attacked 11,980 enemy vehicles, and had destroyed 1,420 of them.

In the 9 May 1951, attack on Sinuiji Airfield, First Marine Air Wing Corsairs and 18th Wing P-51 Mustangs dropped bombs and napalm and also launched rockets against targets in the ten-square-mile airfield area. The attack force destroyed all the communist aircraft on the field, destroyed 106 buildings, fired an unusually large aviation fuel dump, exploded 26 other ammunition and fuel dumps, and undoubtedly inflicted heavy casualties among the ranks of the enemy personnel who streamed out of the buildings.

Design work on a Marine Corps ground attack version of the Corsair, the F4U-6, was initiated by Vought in 1950. On 31 January 1951, the Navy awarded Vought a contract for the new Corsair. This model was designed especially for Korean-type close air support operations, and by the time the first production aircraft flew its maiden flight on 31 January 1952, it had been redesignated the AU-1.

The heavy supercharging equipment required for high-altitude combat operations was eliminated, and instead, the AU-1 was powered by a low-altitude version of the Double Wasp engine, the R-2800-83WA, with a single-stage, two-speed, manually-controlled supercharger. The engine cowl supercharger air inlet ducts were eliminated, and the oil coolers were moved inboard from the air inlet to a position between the wing and fuselage to make the plane less vulnerable to ground fire. Armour plating was added throughout the airplane, which protected the pilot and the undersides of the engine, the engine accessory section, and fuel tanks.

The AU-1's basic armament consisted of four 20-millimetre M-3 automatic cannons. Ten five-inch rockets, six 500lb bombs, or ten 250lb bombs could be carried under the outer wing panels. Bombs weighing up to 1,600lbs, 11.75-inch rockets, or 150-gallon drop tanks could be carried on twin wing centre section pylons. One bomb weighing up to 2,000lbs could be carried on a centreline pylon. The normal gross weight of the AU-1 was the same as the F4U-5, 12,900lbs. A total of 111 AU-1s were produced, the last of which was delivered on 10 October 1952.

In August 1952, Captain Jesse G.

Far left, top: A winterised Corsair night fighter, an F4U-5NL of Navy Composite Squadron VC-35 on board the USS *Antietam* (CVE-36). /US Navy

Far left, centre: A Marine Air Group 11 F4U-5P photo recce Corsair from the USS *Leyte Gulf* (CVE-32) over the island of Isola Ustica, Korea, 9 December 1950. The starboard oblique camera door (below the forward side bars of the national insignia) is open and the pilot is probably photographing the airplane that this photo was shot from. /USMC via Rowland Gill

Far left, bottom: A Marine Utility Squadron VMJ-3 F4U-5P on board the USS *Bairoko* (CVE-115), 5 May 1951. /US Navy via Harold Andrews

Top left: VMF-323 'Death Rattlers' F4U-4B Corsairs at Seoul's Kimpo Airfield, Korea, 29 April 1951. A cannon-armed F4U-4B, loaded down with 5-inch HVARS, two 1000lb bombs and a centre-line drop tank, bogged down as the pilot attempted to move on to the taxiway, and ground crewmen are attempting to rock it free. /USMC via Rowland Gill

Centre left: A VMF-312 'Checkerboard' F4U-4B taxiing past a VMF-214 'Black Sheep' F4U-4. VMF-214 and 312 served together in Korea as part of the First Marine Air Wing. /USMC via Rowland Gill

Below: A VMF-312 'Checkerboard' F4U-4 with a load of 250 and 1000lb bombs about to be catapulted off the USS *Battan* (CVE- 29), 19 May 1952. /US National Archives

Right: Marine F4U-4s loaded with 1000lb bombs and 5-inch HVARS prepare for a strike against North Korean targets. */US National Archives*

Above: VMF-323 'Death Rattlers'
F4U-4Bs, loaded with 250lb
bombs and 5-inch HVARs at
Seoul's Kimpo Airfield, Korea.
/USMC via Rowland Gill

Left: A Marine Utility Squadron
VMJ-3 cannon-armed F4U-4B
over Korea, 18 May 1952.
/USMC via Rowland Gill

Folmar became the first American to shoot down a Russian-built MiG-15 with a propeller-driven fighter, a Corsair. Folmar and his wingman, Lieutenant William Daniels, were looking for targets near the town of Chinnampo when they were jumped by five MiG-15s. One of the jets launched the attack when Folmar noticed red tracers starting to whip past the nose of his airplane. The jet was moving too fast, and shortly thereafter, it slipped in front of Folmar. The MiG was starting to climb as Folmar brought his gun sight to bear on the jet's tailpipe. He pressed on the trigger button and laced 20-millimetre cannon shells into the MiG. Grey smoke started to flow from the rear of the enemy airplane, and it then turned black. The Corsair had scored a kill. Immediately afterwards another MiG badly damaged Folmar's Corsair, but he bailed out and was soon rescued.

Air strikes were continued against enemy targets by US Marine Corps and Navy Corsairs up to the last day of the Korean conflict, 27 July 1953.

Far left, top: VMF-214 'Black Sheep'
F4U-4Bs aboard the USS Sicily
(CVE-118). The cannon-armed
Corsairs are loaded with 5-inch
HVARs and incendiary bombs.
/USMC via Rowland Gill

Far left, bottom: A factory fresh
USMC AU-1 ground attack
version of the Corsair. Although
originally designated the F4U-6,
a change in the designation
system created the AU-1, the first
Vought attack type.
/US National Archives

Above: A VMF-323 'Death
Rattlers' AU-1 Corsair in Korea
with a load of six 500lb and two
1000lb bombs, 20 February 1953.
/USMC via Rowland Gill

Left: F4U-4Bs of VF-113 or 114
with their loads of 5-inch HVARs
and 500lb bombs about to be
launched from the USS
Philippine Sea (CVE-47) a for
strike against North Korean
targets. 5 August 1950.
/US National Archives

Triple Threat Ace
Commander Guy P. Bordelon, Jr., USN (Ret.)

During the Korean campaign, Commander Bordelon (then Lieutenant) became the only 'triple threat' ace of the war by shooting down five enemy aircraft at night. At the time he was serving as officer in charge of Night Composite Squadron Three (VC-3), which was operating on the USS *Princeton*. Records show that he was the only US Navy ace of the Korean conflict, the only ace who flew propeller fighters, and the only night fighter ace. Falling before his guns in night combat were two Yakolev (Yak-18) intruder bombers, and three Lavochkin (LA-11) fighters of the communist forces. Commander Bordelon describes his night fighter experiences in Korea.

"Let us speak briefly about the Corsair. The model which we used in Korea was the F4U-5N, designed specifically for use as a night fighter and was at that time the hottest version of the Corsair. Our bird was an R2800-32W engine, which, although capable of producing considerably more power, was throttle-stopped at 2,300hp.

"It was equipped with an APS-19A radar, which was a development of the old WW II APS-4 and APS-6 radars. The APS-19A had an excellent range in search, an excellent range in beacon, and a fair range in the intercept mode. Fair at that time was something like three and one-half miles. This was with the gear at its very best. Most of the time, it was good for about two and one-half miles.

"For armament we had four 20mm cannon and could carry 12 bombs on the wings or eight bombs on the wings plus two centreline bombs. Our missions were four to four and a half hours long which necessitated carrying a 150-gallon auxiliary fuel tank. Additionally, on one of the centreline racks we carried a 500lb bomb. On the outboard wing racks we usually carried 250lb bombs equipped with daisy-cutter fuzes.

"Our primary targets were the interdiction type — trucks and trains. Since we were bombing at night we wanted a bomb that had the greatest area of dispersal when it exploded. The 250lb bomb with the daisy-cutter fuze was ideal for this purpose. Use of the 500lb bomb was not too satisfactory. Despite every effort, we were unable to ensure better than a 70 per cent detonation rate, most likely because both the bombs and fuzes had been manufactured during WW II and were just too old to do the job.

"The 20mm cannon was our most effective weapon. It could be used against any type of target and was very flexible. We carried 200 rounds per gun and normally fired down to a 50-round low limit per gun. Although we had standard loads issued by Task Force 77, the choice of ammo was generally left to the crew. Our recommendations were given every consideration by the Admiral and he was most responsive to our suggestions. My personal choice was a full load of HEI (high explosive incendiary) since the trucks were carrying incendiary type loads of fuel, ammunition and other supplies. We found this to be a most effective weapon.

"One of the problems unique to the Corsair was the length of its nose, thus giving rise to its popular nickname — the Hose Nose. At sundry times it has also been known as the U-Bird, Bent-Wing Monster, and Ensign Eliminator, to name but a few. But the long nose was the feature that gave the pilots the most difficulty. This difficulty was evident during night carrier landings when it seemed to the pilot that he had 40 feet of nose sticking out in front of him. Fortunately, the Corsair was equipped with flame dampeners to hide the flame from the exhaust stacks. This was a great help in coming aboard at night. But since we were landing aboard an axial deck carrier, the angle deck not yet being in vogue, it became a matter of being able to see the LSO. Not having the mirror at that time, every landing was a thrill, especially on nights when we had a light mist or a slight hydraulic leak (which was common to most Corsairs). My personal choice of landing technique, and one I think most pilots used, was to be in a continuous turn up to the last second with a very short straightaway so you could see the LSO at all times.

"Most of us preferred a catapult launch in this bird, although as a rule prop aircraft were still being launched with a deck run. The reasoning for this was simple — the F4U-5N had an automatic engine control unit which required time to arm. In some planes it took as long as 11 seconds to become fully armed. This meant that on deck launches, the pilot had to hold maximum power as long as possible without digging the prop into the deck before releasing the brakes to start the takeoff run. On several occasions I didn't get full power until two-thirds of the way down the deck and almost 'dribbled' off the bow. The cat shot was always a good solid feeling. One disadvantage that did occur on catapult shots was caused by bridle slap punching holes in the auxiliary fuel tanks. This did make for shorter hops!

"Early in 1953 our Task Force got a call saying that Admiral Jocko Clark had put us on the line. The Air Force had been complaining that they were losing some of their F-94Cs. This was an all-weather version of the old F-80. These squadrons of F-94Cs had been charged with intercepting the enemy night intruder aircraft used to bomb the cities, particularly Seoul and Inchon. The Air Force had not been successful in stopping them. One squadron apparently lost the CO, executive officer, and operations officer by flying into mountains due to the fact that their aircraft were too fast to intercept the relatively slow flying prop aircraft such as the YAK-18, LA-11, and the two old TU-2 bombers. The communists had been most successful in their efforts and just before Admiral Clark made the call to our Task Force, had bombed Inchon destroying some 15 million gallons of aviation fuel and other supplies. The Air Force bemoaned this fact and Admiral Clark responded, 'We have just the aircraft and pilots for you and they're eager to do the job. Our Corsair night fighters are out aboard ship and they can fly as slow as is necessary.'

"General Anderson, who was Commanding General of the Fifth Air Force in Korea, invited us to come in. Four of us flew in to K-14 airfield, which was just south of Seoul and were briefed by the Air Force and by Joint Operations Centre, Korea. Then we were shifted to K-16 field about 50 miles south of Seoul. Our CAP (Combat Air Patrol) barrier was just south of the bomb line which had been established at the armistice talks then going on.

"On the third night of operations I was scrambled to counter unidentified slow-flying aircraft which were closing in on our base of operations. Under the control of the base GCA controller, I was vectored into radar contact with these aircraft. The enemy pilots performed many evasive manoeuvres at airspeeds of from 80 to 130 knots which resulted in a long hard struggle for me to get within visual range. After about 45 minutes, however, I was able to obtain a visual and by frequent use of the flaps, varying airspeed from 90 to 160 knots, was able to close to firing position. Upon opening fire on the enemy aircraft, a YAK-18, hits were observed and the enemy rolled to the left, diving straight into the water from an altitude of about 800 feet.

"The second kill was obtained in much the same way, with the difference being that as the first burst was fired, return fire was received from the rear cockpit of the enemy plane. After a second long burst was fired into him, the enemy aircraft, another YAK-18, crashed and burned.

"Two nights later, while on barrier patrol north of Seoul, the radar controller reported many unidentified aircraft headed south toward Seoul. When vectored on one group, radar contact was established on a loose formation of three aircraft. When contact was reported the formation split, and I concentrated on one of them, chasing him some 30 miles before being able to close to firing range. Identifying the aircraft by silhouette as an enemy LA-11 fighter, I opened fire from close astern observing his left wing tearing off, then crashing beneath me.

"Vectored on another group of unidentified aircraft by the Seoul controller, contact was soon established and the chase was on. For about 10 minutes a single aircraft was chased at all altitudes and airspeeds over land and water until finally well north of enemy lines, visual contact was established with an enemy LA-11 fighter. Shortly after fire was opened, the enemy began to burn, and as fire was continued, he spun into the water where he continued to burn for approximately 20 seconds.

"The Korean experience was most interesting and rewarding. The Corsair came through beautifully; she was a sturdy old bird, one that we all loved. None of these kills would have been possible had it not been for the excellent manoeuvrability and great range of airspeeds available with the Corsair."

Corsairs with the French Navy

A group of Aéronavale (French Naval Air Arm) pilots made their first flights in the new F4U-7 version of the Corsair at Naval Air Station Oceana, Virginia, on 24 October 1952. After approximately six weeks of training there, the pilots went aboard the French carrier *Lafayette* with 45 F4U-7s, their final destination the French Naval Base at Bizerte, a Tunisian port on the Mediterranean Sea.

The F4U-7 was specifically designed for operation by Aéronavale close air support and attack squadrons in Indo China. The F4U-7 version was basically an F4U-4 in an AU-1 airframe, and was powered by the same R-2800-18W engine used in the early F4U-4s. The F4U-7 first flew on 2 July 1952, and the last of the 94 airplanes that were supplied to France under the Military Defense Assistance Programme was delivered on 31 January 1953.

On 18 April 1954, 25 AU-1s were delivered to the Aéronavale in fly-away condition at Da Nang. These aircraft were reportedly from VMA-211 and Marine Air Group 12. Later, an additional unknown number of AU-1s were given to the Aéronavale for their use in the Indo China War. The Aéronavale Corsair squadrons operated over Dien Bien Phu, in the Tonkin Mountains and over the Tonkin Gulf until the fall of Dien Bien Phu on 7 May 1954.

Later, action came in Algeria. The first combat operations involving the Aéronavale Corsair squadrons were flown on 10-19 May 1956. In October 1956, Aéronavale Corsair squadrons aboard the carriers *Arromanches* and *Lafayette* were used to help defend the Suez Canal during the 1956 Arab - Israeli War. The Aéronavale Corsair squadrons continued operating in Algeria until France finally granted her independence in July 1962.

The Aéronavale Corsairs were called into action at Bizerte in August 1963, to help defend the strategic base. A short time later, they helped cover the evacuation operations there when Tunisia demanded that France withdraw its troops and give up its Tunisian bases.

Below: A Flotille 12F AU-1 Corsair at Telergma, Algeria, January 1960./*Jim Sullivan*

Top right: A F4U-7 Corsair during a company test flight near Dallas, Texas. /*Vought Aircraft via Art Schoeni*

Bottom right: These Aéronavale AU-1s are in various stages of having markings applied and are believed to have been assigned to Flotille 14F in Indo China. /*Establissement Cinématographique et Photographique des Armées — ECA*

Above: Aéronavale ground crewmen preparing Flotille 14F AU-1s for a strike in Indo China.
/ECA via Bernard Millot

Right: Flotille 14F AU-1s on a bombing mission in Indo China.
/ECA via Bernard Millot

Far right: Flotille 14F AU-1 Corsairs loaded with 500lb bombs in Indo China.
/ECA via Bernard Millot

Above: A Flotille 12F F4U-7 during a training mission. /ECA via Bernard Millot

Centre right: Flotille 14F F4U-7 Corsair prepare for takeoff from the French carrier *Arromanches*. /Service Cinéma des Armées

Below right: An F4U-7 Corsair assigned to Flotille 15F. /ECA

Far right, top: Flotille 14F F4U-7 Corsairs aboard an unknown French carrier, February 1954. /ECA

Far right, bottom: A Flotille 14F F4U-7 landing aboard an unknown French carrier. /ECA via Bernard Millot